# Hugo Blanco

To my mother Yvonne Wall

# Hugo Blanco
## A revolutionary for life

DEREK WALL

Resistance Books
MERLIN PRESS

First published in 2018
by The Merlin Press
Central Books Building
Freshwater Road
London
RM8 1RX

www.merlinpress.co.uk

in association with Resistance Books
www.resistancebooks.org

British Library Cataloguing in Publication Data
is available from the British Library

ISBN 978-0-85036-748-5

Printed in the UK by Imprint Digital, Exeter

# Contents

# Acknowledgements

There are many people to thank. First and foremost Hugo himself, ever supportive, despite being a busy person he responded with corrections and suggestions at all stages of writing. My wife Emily Blyth read every word with care, putting in hours to make my writing comprehensible, my love and thanks for her constant support. Terry Conway equally put immense work into the text, which is greatly appreciated, Terry has made sure this book happened and has my deep gratitude. Christine Smith translated Hugo's discussion of Cusco with an 'S', while Vincent Wall helped knock Chapter Three into shape. Anthony Zurbrugg at Merlin Press greeted the idea of this book with great enthusiasm, I must thank him for making it possible. Christopher K. Starr sent me his translations of 140 editorials written by Hugo for *Lucha Indigena*, this was a very great help. Ian Angus, Gunilla Berglund, Ana Blanco, Jaymie Patricia Heilman, Adrian Howe, Romayne Phoenix and Jason Travis all gave vital support. Oscar Blanco Berglund for many conversations and support.

The mistakes are all mine and the wisdom is entirely Hugo's.

## Cusco with an 'S'

I received this comment from Hugo after sending him a first draft of Chapter Two. Redrafting, I have used 'Cusco' except where it has been written with a 'z' in passages I am quoting. *Tawantinsuyu* refers to what is often wrongly termed the 'Inca Empire'. I have used the term *Tawantinsuyu* after the point I discuss this in the text, so as to avoid confusion.

I've seen that at times you write Cusco with an S. This is the history of the name: It was the capital of *Tawantinsuyu* (The Four Regions) which was called Qosqo (which means centre or navel). In the Quechua language, there are three vowels: A; one which is somewhere between E and I – and another between O and U, so that when Quechua is written in Spanish, either vowel may be used. The 'Z' sound of Castilian Spanish spoken in mainland Spain doesn't exist in Quechua (neither does it in Latin American Spanish). Neither does Castilian Spanish have the sound of the Quechua consonant 'Q', and so in its place, 'C' is written. Because 'S' exists in both languages, Qosqo thus becomes Cusco. So then, why is it that a Z is used so that we get Cuzco? It is used to humiliate us, because in the Castilian Spanish dictionary, 'cuzco' means 'small barking dog'. And thus a mayor of Cusco passed a ruling that Cusco should be written with an S. I write it this way and was surprised to note that you too also sometimes use this spelling.

(Hugo Blanco comment July 2018)

# Timeline

| | |
|---|---|
| 1934 | Hugo Blanco born in Cusco |
| 1944 | meets the indigenous leader Lorenzo Chamorro |
| 1951 | involved in school protest against a principal imposed by dictatorial government |
| 1954 | university student in Argentina, demonstrates against coup in Guatemala |
| 1955 | works in a meat packing factory, active as a Trotskyist around the group publishing *Palabra Obrera* (Workers Word) in La Plata |
| 1957 | returns to Peru, works in factory, organises politically in Lima |
| 1958 | participates in the demonstration against Richard Nixon, US Vice-President |
| 1958 | returns to Cusco because of political persecution |
| April 1958 | becomes a sub-tenant farmer |
| 1958-63 | organises peasants of Lares and La Convención |
| 1963-66 | trial and imprisonment |
| 1966-70 | imprisoned in El Frontón |
| 1971 | exiled to Mexico |
| 1972 | travels to Argentina and is imprisoned, moves to Chile |
| 1973-75 | exile in Sweden |
| 1975 | returns to Peru but is exiled back to Sweden |
| 1978 | elected to Constituent Assembly but deported to Argentina |
| 1980 | candidate for Peruvian Presidency |

| | |
|---|---|
| 1980–85 | serves in Peruvian Congress |
| 1986 | moves to Puno, active in land struggles |
| 1987 | works in Piura supporting peasants |
| 1989 | works in Ucayali region, witnessed massacre of strikers |
| 1990 | elected as Senator, serves on the environment committee |
| 1992 | escapes to Mexico, after death threats from security services and Shining Path |
| 1993–1997 | lives in Mexico |
| 1997 | returns to Peru |
| 2002 | brain surgery |
| 2006 | starts publishing *Lucha Indigena* |
| 2008 | arrested in land dispute |
| 2009 | active in supporting the Bagua uprising in the Amazon |
| 2010 | speaking tour in Britain during which Hugo meets Jeremy Corbyn. Publication of *Nosotros los Indios* (We the Indians) Ediciones La Minga, Buenos Aires, Argentina. |
| 2016 | Hugo Blanco Galdos School for Environmental and Social Leaders established in Peru as a resource for anti-mining activists |
| 2017 | demonstrates against pardoning of Fujimori |

# Introduction

Hugo Blanco, born in 1934, has been an active revolutionary for almost his entire life. There are, however, at least two Hugo Blancos. I don't mean that Hugo Blanco is both the name of a well-known Venezuelan musician, famous for compositions such as *Moliendo Café* and *Leche Condensada*, and the Peruvian radical who is subject of this book. Hugo Blanco has had two revolutionary lives – as both a committed Marxist inspired by Lenin and Trotsky and as a radical indigenous leader. Hugo, while some of us his views have evolved over time, sees no contradiction between these two sources of radical inspiration.

He started at high school, joining a mutiny to remove a new principal imposed by the right-wing Peruvian government. Described as the 'Fidel Castro of the Andes', like Fidel and Che, he was a charismatic revolutionary during the 1960s (Feuer 1969: 247). Beginning to write this book in December 2017, I saw him on video, addressing a crowd of thousands protesting in Lima against the pardoning of former President Fujimori. Fujimori's crimes included the forced sterilisation of indigenous women. The protests helped remove the sitting President Pedro Pablo Kuczynski from office in March 2018 and Fujimori is being tried once again for human rights abuse. Hugo Blanco's story is one of continuous, thoughtful militancy.

It was said that 'in every peasant's home there is an empty bed', kept in case Hugo Blanco needed it on his return to the Andes. During the 1960s, devotion to Hugo, who had helped the peasants to occupy their land and expel the hated *gamonales*, the abusive landowners, was 'total' (Neira translated by Maitan 1965: 40). While Neira, a Peruvian journalist, was writing in the 1960s, Hugo is still held in great affection in indigenous communities today:

> In the Peruvian Sierra, Hugo Blanco has legendary status. Children and teenagers have heard his name discussed, and many were able to tell me of his exploits. Touring the mountains around Pisac, Calca and Urumbamba, an area called the Sacred Valley of the Inca, Blanco is constantly stopped and thanked, asked about his health, and invariably told news of the local

political situation. His opinion is sought, not only for political analyses but, as has become clear to me after observing his reception at political congresses across Latin America, for methodological direction in the strategic development of social movements. (Ward 2011: 651)

As the English Marxist historian Eric Hobsbawm observed, Hugo Blanco helped 'the most important peasant movement of that period in Peru, and probably in the whole of South America' (1969: 31). This suggests some strategic acumen. Although he was captured and imprisoned, the uprising he led succeeded, the big estates were broken up and the indigenous gained the land they demanded. Hugo Blanco has often, throughout his long decades of engagement, propelled the campaigns he has supported to victory. From helping children selling newspapers to gain higher pay (1959), to aiding local farmers halt huge mining projects in the 2010s in Northern Peru, he can be seen as a successful social movement organiser. These local struggles reflect a wider history of mobilisations in Latin America, with elite groups oppressing the mass of the population and exploiting the environment since the Spanish invasions of the sixteenth century, being met with often fierce resistance. The history of revolutions and radicalism since the 1950s in Latin America can be understood from the perspective of Hugo Blanco, from demonstrating against the 1954 coup in Guatemala, to debating with supporters of Castro and Che, to witnessing first-hand the CIA backed coup against Allende in Chile in 1973, via the Maoist Shining Path's bloody war in the 1980s and 1990s, to encountering the Zapatistas and the electoral left of Hugo Chavez and Evo Morales. It is possible to write a history of the left in Latin America from the 1950s to today based on much of Hugo's life experience.

This, in turn, can be linked to the trajectory of Trotskyism, not just in Latin America but globally. While Hugo Blanco has since rejected some of Trotskyism, during the 1960s and 1970s he was lauded as an inspiring Trotskyist leader. In turn, many of his concerns, particularly the endorsement of ecosocialism, seem to prefigure more recent developments within Trotskyism. While the legacy of Trotsky is disputed and there are numerous groups, parties and internationals, often locked in intense mutual conflict, perhaps the best known and largest, the Fourth International, formerly the United Secretariat of the Fourth International, closely observes Hugo Blanco's work (Fourth International 1996). They declared themselves ecosocialists in 2010, are committed to open and inclusive political work and see the contributions of peasants and indigenous peoples as essential to practical twenty-first century Marxist politics (Thornett 2010). Despite differences, members of the Fourth International and Hugo Blanco retain respect and dialogue in 2018.

Increasingly, Hugo Blanco's concern is with the politics of ecological survival; he argues we 'have reached a point where the private ownership of the means of production has turned into the private ownership of the means of destruction'. (Olivera 2011). He has much to say to Marxists and revolutionaries of different colours, but he is also a key thinker for all of us who advocate green politics. Ecological politics is essential; if we wreck the environment we also threaten the future of humanity. A bleak script seems to be being written. Climate change is producing extreme weather conditions, emissions of $CO_2$ and other greenhouse gases continue to rise, yet denial is deepening. At the same time right-wing populists, most notably Donald Trump, are attacking even the mildest and most ineffective forms of environmental protection. Environmental crisis is creating refugees, and those seeking refuge are often demonised to fuel racist reaction and cement the power of right-wing populist leaders. It is easy to point out what it is wrong, but these immense challenges require precise, effective and, I would suggest, militant action to reverse the damage.

Hugo Blanco's life is fascinating but most significant perhaps is his continuous militancy and careful thought about practical political action. His approach is vital in informing what we do now in the early decades of the twenty-first century to combat a crisis that is ecological, economic, social and political. Both the Trotskyist and the indigenous elements of his politics have fuelled his resistance. This book, above all, aims to explore Hugo Blanco's contribution to potential 'strategic developments' in the light of climate change and right-wing populist reaction.

Chapter One explains how I came to meet Hugo, examines some of the influences on his thought and provides a brief description of the Peruvian context when he was born in 1934.

Chapter Two examines Hugo's family background, childhood and early activism covering the years between 1934 and 1958. Hugo was born in Cusco, the former *Tawantinsuyu* capital city, and could speak Quechua, a language of the indigenous people of the Andes. His political activism started at school but was deepened when he became a student in Argentina. A Trotskyist, he left university and immersed himself in political activity including trade union activism. Returning to Peru, he took part in a major protest against the visit of the then US Vice President Richard Nixon.

Chapter Three examines the events around the La Convención uprising for which Hugo is best known and covers the period from 1958 to 1962. Hugo became a subtenant farmer in the Convención Valley and organised a trade union to fight for the peasants. This was attacked by landowners, so Hugo organised a self-defence force and the peasants began to occupy land.

Matters accelerated, and a full-scale uprising occurred. He was at the time leader of the Campesino Confederation of Peru (CCP). On the run from the police and the army, Hugo was captured in 1963.

Chapter Four deals with Hugo's prison experience and takes the story up to 1970. On trial and threatened with the death penalty, Hugo was sentenced to 25 years in prison, being sent to the bleak island of El Frontón. A huge international campaign for his freedom ended with his release in 1970.

Chapter Five looks at the years between 1970 and 1973. Much of Latin America was coming under the control of right-wing military dictators. These were years of exile, with Hugo living variously in Mexico, Argentina, Chile and Sweden. Hugo witnessed the coup against Allende in Chile and was lucky to have escaped execution by the right-wing Pinochet regime.

Chapter Six covers the period between 1973 and 1992. Returning to Peru, Hugo was elected to congress, ran for President and later became a Senator. He became increasingly concerned with environmental problems as well as social injustice. The political situation became more dangerous; with both the Maoist Shining Path and Peru's internal security force threatening to kill him, Hugo left Peru and moved to Mexico.

Chapter Seven focuses on the importance of the Zapatistas to Hugo's political thinking. Living in Mexico he came into contact with the Zapatistas who launched an uprising in the southern Chiapas state in 1994. This chapter looks at the years 1992 to 2002.

Chapter Eight brings the story up to 2018. Since returning to Peru, Hugo has plunged into the indigenous struggles, campaigns to protect nature and has published *Lucha Indígena*.

Chapter Nine concludes with an examination of Hugo's political perspectives and the application of these to continuing social change.

1

# 'Hugo Blanco has set an example'

'Our only hope of salvation lies in breaking down this economic system and replacing it with another that is governed by humanity as a whole and not a handful of millionaires.' Hugo Blanco (2010b)

Interviewed in Algeria in July 1963 Che Guevara had this to say about Hugo Blanco:

Hugo Blanco is the head of one of the guerrilla movements in Peru. He struggled stubbornly but the repression was strong. I don't know what his tactics of struggle were, but his fall does not signify the end of the movement. It is only a man that has fallen, but the movement continues. One time, when we were preparing to make our landing from the *Granma*, and when there was a great risk that all of us would be killed, Fidel said: 'What is more important than us is the example we set.' It's the same thing. Hugo Blanco has set an example, a good example, and he struggled as much as he could. (quoted in Gott 1973: 373)

Hugo Blanco led a peasant uprising to gain land rights in the early 1960s in Peru. As noted by Che, he was captured in 1963 and his prosecutors sought the death penalty. Unlike Che who was killed in Bolivia, the country neighbouring Peru, in 1967, Hugo Blanco survived his guerrilla days.

If we fast forward to September 2010, we find Hugo in North London speaking at a book launch. This event is chaired by Hugo's son Oscar Blanco Berglund who introduces another speaker, Jeremy Corbyn. Oscar describes him as the Labour Party's second most rebellious MP. Jeremy corrects him, insisting that he is in fact the most rebellious, voting against his party more often than any other Labour parliamentarian. Jeremy Corbyn was elected leader of the Labour Party in 2015 and has transformed his party in a left direction, radicalising British politics in the process. Hugo Blanco continues to set an example; praised by Che in the 1960s, we find him on a platform with Jeremy Corbyn fifty years later.

Hugo has been a consistent and determined fighter for indigenous rights. Eduardo Galeano, the Uruguayan journalist and novelist, often described as a literary giant of Latin America, argued that Hugo Blanco was born twice:

> The first time was in Cuzco in 1934.
> Hugo Blanco arrived in a country split in two, Peru.
> He was born somewhere in between.
> He was white, but he was raised in a town, Huanoquite, where the mates he played and ran with spoke Quechua, and he went to school in Cuzco, where the pavements were reserved for decent folk, and Indians were not allowed on them.
> Hugo was born the second time when he was ten years old. In school he heard the news from his town that Don Bartolomé Paz had branded an Indian peon named Francisco Zamata with a red-hot iron. This owner of lands and people had seared his initials, BP, on the peon's behind because he hadn't taken good care of his cows.
> The matter was not so uncommon, but it branded Hugo for life.
> Over the years, this man who was not Indian became one. He organized peasant unions and paid the price for his self-chosen disgrace with beatings and torture, jail and harassment and exile.
> On one of his fourteen hunger strikes, when he could go on no longer, the government was so moved it sent him a coffin as a present.
> (Galeano 2013: 15)

Hugo Blanco has lived through a series of dramatic events; his story is part of the continuing struggles of the people of Latin Americas for liberation and hope. As a boy he witnessed oppression and dictatorship in Peru, he was a student in Argentina when Perón was removed by a coup. After leading a combative movement for land rights, he spent much of the 1960s in the bleak island prison of El Frontón. He was an exile in Chile when the socialist government of Salvador Allende was destroyed by General Pinochet and the CIA in 1973.

Eventually returning from exile in Sweden, he was first elected as a member of the Constituent Assembly, later as a member of Congress and finally as a Senator. Hugo also ran for President in Peru in 1980. Much of Hugo's life has been marked by repression; he has suffered numerous arrests, beatings, years in exile, and has cheated death on numerous occasions. Placed on death lists by both the Maoist organisation the Shining Path and Peru's official state security apparatus, he had to leave Peru in 1992.

Living in Mexico, Hugo was powerfully influenced by the example of the Zapatistas, a revolutionary movement that erupted in the southern part of the country in 1994. They rejected both the electoral strategies of the left and the Leninist concept of building a disciplined revolutionary party which would take power. Instead of taking power, they sought to build power directly through building their own community, independent from the state. They advocated horizontal rather than hierarchical structures and embraced indigenous culture. Since 2006, Hugo has published the newspaper *Lucha Indigena* (Indigenous Struggle), supporting indigenous communities fighting for their future and advocating a Zapatista type vision of social change.

Hugo's solidarity extends beyond Peru. Recently visiting Greece, he met those challenging austerity:

> In Greece, I've seen that in face of the government austerity, there's a rise in activity from the base. For example, the government abandoned the state television channel and in Thessaloniki the workers took it in their power and they interviewed me. Later, because they were closing clinics, health workers – nurses and doctors – met up and made clinics. There is also a publishing house in the hands of its workers. There are many restaurants in Athens that are in the hands of their workers. There is a cooperative that receives goods from the countryside and sells them, avoiding intermediaries. And I told them, 'You're doing here in the city what the Zapatistas are doing in the countryside: creating power'. (Hamilton 2017)

In 2009 he wrote to thank workers on the Isle of Wight in Britain who had occupied their factory, attempting to defend jobs at Vestas, a wind turbine manufacturer threatened with closure:

> Recently, in Peru, indigenous ecologists were massacred by the government, which was acting in support of large multinational companies devastating the Amazon rain forest. This has shaken us and made us more aware of any act of environmental destruction.
>
> We are in solidarity with those, in whatever part of the world, who defend the wellbeing of the planet. For that reason we totally support the workers of Vestas Wind Turbine on the Isle of Wight who have occupied their factory.
>
> From the other side of the world, we ask those who are closer than us to support these workers by all necessary means. We hope that all the inhabitants of the planet will express to them the gratitude that they deserve. (Socialist Resistance 2009)

In recent decades, Hugo has sought to promote ecosocialist politics, linking Latin American struggles, often based on localised struggles against environmental damage, to global ecological concerns. With the crisis of neoliberal globalisation, a new generation of political activists are emerging across the planet. Hugo Blanco has much to say in the context of a thirst to make a politics of liberation less Eurocentric, less hierarchical and more diverse and ecological.

Hugo is, in 2018, both militant and undogmatic. He has shown considerable strategic and tactical flexibility in his politics, he rejects the idea that one political method is universally correct, stressing that a close attention to context is vital. He notes that labels like Marxism or anarchism are often fought over, but practical analysis to inform specific action should be the role of theory, rather than loyalty to a specific ideological description. While clear concepts matter, they should not be a source of sectarianism; the revolution involves cooperation as well as clarity.

In this Chapter I will discuss how I came to meet Hugo Blanco, examine some of the influences on his thought, provide a brief description of the Peruvian context when he was born in 1934 and outline the remainder of this book.

## Meeting Hugo

I have been active in the green movement since 1980, variously contesting elections, taking occasional direct action and agitating for ecological causes. I have written a number of books on green politics, socialism and the commons. My connection with Hugo started when I used his words. I had no idea who he was, but I read and was captured by a passage he wrote about ecological politics. I recycled it to introduce a chapter I had written in my book on anti-capitalist economics, *Babylon and Beyond*:

> There are in Peru a very large number of people who are environmentalists. Of course, if I tell such people, you are ecologists, they might reply, 'ecologist your mother' or words to that effect. Let us see, however. Isn't the village of Bambamarca truly environmentalist, which has time and again fought valiantly against the pollution of its water from mining? Are not the town of Ilo and the surrounding villages which are being polluted by the Southern Peru Copper Corporation truly environmentalist? Is not the village of Tambo Grande in Piura environmentalist when it rises like a closed fist and is ready to die in order to prevent strip-mining in its valley? (Blanco quoted in Wall 2005: 153-154)

In December 2007 I was enjoying a beer with my friend the Canadian ecosocialist Ian Angus in The George, a positively Dickensian pub in Southwark, London. Supping our pints, we had much to say to each other. Ian told me that he knew Hugo Blanco, from his days as a Trotskyist in the 1970s and 1980s. Since then I have kept in email contact with Hugo.

In 2008, much to my surprise, I was contacted by Hugo's son Oscar, who lives in Britain, to say that Hugo was in prison and asking if I could help to free him. I made my small contribution to the campaign, emailing Members of Parliament and activists. Arrested as part of a struggle for land rights, Hugo was happily quickly released.

Hugo has been a key supporter of international networks for ecosocialism. Ecosocialism, as the name denotes, is a fusion of socialist and ecological politics. Ecosocialists argue that ecological problems are produced by a capitalist economic system that requires ever more consumption, production and waste (Löwy 2015). Especially since the 1990s, Hugo has argued that ecological problems impact on indigenous people and peasants affected, as noted above, by pollution and mining. In turn, he suggests that indigenous struggles to resist the extraction of fossil fuels, and to defend forests and other essential ecosystems, are vital in challenging climate change and other ecological dangers that threaten the whole of humanity. Hugo was kind enough to write the foreword to my book on ecosocialism *The Rise of the Green Left* (Wall 2010).

In 2010 two ecosocialist organisations, Green Left and Socialist Resistance, organised a speaking tour in Britain for Hugo. Green Left is the anti-capitalist network in the Green Party of England and Wales. Socialist Resistance is a British organisation which collaborates with Trotsky's Fourth International. While Hugo no longer defines himself as a Trotskyist, he retains an affection for the Fourth International. Despite being in his seventies, he addressed packed meetings in London, Birmingham, Bristol, Cardiff, Manchester and Edinburgh with great energy and enthusiasm.

I met Hugo at Heathrow airport. He was easy to spot, with his trademark medical hat and full white beard. He suffered severe brain injury as a result of various police beatings and was treated in Mexico and Cuba. His broad brimmed straw hat helps to protect his head from accidental knocks. Hugo speaks fluent Quechua, Spanish and Swedish but little English; my Spanish is limited but we had numerous conversations during our stay. On political matters, discussing Bolivar or Trotsky, we understood each other. On practical matters, such as arranging when to take a taxi to Heathrow for his return flight, confusion reigned.

Between 2012 and 2017, I took on the role of International Coordinator of the Green Party of England and Wales; a key aim was to promote Hugo's work to Green Parties and to provide international solidarity to indigenous peoples. In fact, the solidarity I was able to give proved limited. Positively, much of my energy went into work to defend Rojava. Rojava (the name is Kurdish for the west), is an area of Northern Syria operating under autonomous Kurdish control. In the midst of civil war and the battle against the so-called Islamic State, the Kurds and their allies have built a secular, feminist and democratic republic, based on the ideas of the social ecologist Murray Bookchin (Knapp *et al* 2016). Hugo has been a strong supporter of the Rojava revolution.

Much of my time was taken organising the Global Greens Congress held in Liverpool in 2017 and attending similar international Green Party events. While Green Parties can do important work, it is clear that much serious green politics is a product of grassroots social movements, of the kind with which Hugo is so deeply involved.

Another project to promote green politics that I have been intensely occupied with has been to spread the words and wisdom of Elinor Ostrom, as I write, the only woman so far to have won a Nobel Prize for economics. I have written three books about her work to defend the commons, forms of collective ownership which promote ecological sustainability (Wall 2014a, 2014b and 2017). Having met Elinor in 2012 shortly before her death, it struck me how both she and Hugo are similar characters, with a shared commitment to ecology, self-governance and the indigenous. Both are strikingly iconic and the stuff of legends, a guerrilla leader from the Andes, a Nobel Prize winner from California, yet both are also open, undogmatic and pretty much happy to talk to anybody. I have been lucky enough to have spent time with both, although only briefly with Elinor, and to learn from them. Hugo has praised Elinor's work on the commons and in promotion of indigenous principles (Blanco in Wall 2010a: xi).

Ostrom's work was based on careful social science and promoted the idea that we could cooperate for a better world (Ostrom 1990). Hugo's continuing work retains this vision, but he notes that the rich and the powerful distort human progress, and that ecological problems are a product of an oppressive economic and social system. He reminds us that human liberation and an ecological future demand that we engage in focused but powerful struggles. I would argue that Ostrom and Hugo Blanco complement each other's work, providing a sophisticated basis for green politics.

## Hugo and us

Hugo's story is vivid. Famous in the 1960s, Hugo Blanco sets an example for us today. By us, I mean political activists on the left in Latin America and beyond. I am not looking to write the definitive guide to exactly what Hugo did and thought at various stages in his life; I am interested quite specifically in how his work can inform struggles continuing today. Brecht said that 'Art is not a mirror held up to society, but a hammer with which to shape it'. (Brecht 1964: 425). Biography, if it is political, is about production, producing a better world, not just providing accurate, attractive or even critical portrayal.

The context of politics for left activists has changed dramatically in recent years. Neoliberal globalisation, based on an alliance between governments and corporations, has increasingly lost its appeal. The assumption that by deregulating markets and promoting business, economic growth would bring prosperity to all has been strongly challenged. A globalised economy has brought material benefits for some, but it has also concentrated wealth and accelerated environmental problems, most significantly in the form of climate change. During the 1990s and the first decade of the twenty-first century, the end of history thesis that there was no alternative to mixed but mainly market-based economies seemed to have been borne out. However, the election of Latin American left governments was perhaps a first sign that socialism was re-emerging. While right-wing populists have grown stronger, there is a generation of new left activists growing across the world. In Britain, Jeremy Corbyn, who as was noted earlier is familiar with Hugo Blanco, has moved the Labour Party leftwards and has strong sympathy for ecosocialism. The huge vote for the socialist candidate Bernie Sanders in the 2016 Presidential primaries and the recent growth of the far-left organisation, the Democratic Socialists of America (DSA), point in the same direction.

As we have noted, Hugo's promotion of an egalitarian and ecological future can provide inspiration for those new to socialism and seeking a better world. Given his long-standing promotion of grassroots community power, his politics provides an alternative to a variety of centralised forms of state socialism that have been seen as failures. Hugo equally embraces a feminist politics, noting that right-wing forces are attacking women both in Peru and globally:

The most combative popular movement in the world today is women's struggle against patriarchal society. In his celebrated work on *The Origin of the Family, Private Property and the State*, Marx's collaborator Friedrich Engels stated clearly that 'The first oppressed class is woman'.

He further noted:

> All of us, both women and men, grew up in male-dominated communities, so that the machismo that surrounds us is taken for granted. I, myself, have the good fortune that my daughters, my granddaughters, my partner and other women in my daily life are prepared to point out any lingering male-chauvinist attitudes on my part, so that I can correct them. (Blanco 2018b: 2)

The crisis of the present economic and social model of neoliberal capitalism provides opportunities to change human society including challenging patriarchy. Yet this crisis has been exploited perhaps most effectively by a new populist right wing, most notably with the election of Donald Trump as US President. Trump and similar figures have sought to roll back environmental and social protection, to strengthen nationalism and to harvest insecurity so as to produce yet more racism, misogyny and allied forms of hate.

Hugo's patient but militant activism can help inform strategic thinking on the left, challenging those like Trump, opposing neoliberalism and building an ecological, democratic, diverse and equal future. This book describes his varied experiences of electoral politics, armed struggle, institution building and non-violent direct action to inform efforts to transform our collective future.

In 2002 a fundraising appeal was made on behalf of Hugo, then aged 67, for money for an urgent brain operation, necessary because of injuries he has received at various times during his tumultuous life. Happily, the appeal and the operation were both successful. As part of the appeal he wrote a brief autobiography noting:

> You ask me for a summary of my life. I believe the interesting thing about it is the lessons I learned in the various important situations that I had the good fortune to experience. Unfortunately all this cannot be conveyed in a summary. If I come out of this current adventure alive, I must write about it. (Blanco 2018a: 13)

This book aims to provide one account of such lessons. There are alternative interpretations, but Hugo Blanco's lessons, however interpreted, provide much material on how to resist and build. Hugo's thinking was influenced by the context in which he has lived, and by particular thinkers. The next section outlines the importance of Trotsky, Mariátegui and Arguedas to his political development.

## Influences: Trotsky, Mariategui and Arguedas

Three individuals appear to have had a strong influence on Hugo's early thinking; the Russian revolutionary Leon Trotsky (1879-1940), the Peruvian Marxist José Carlos Mariátegui (1894-1930) and the novelist José María Arguedas (1911-1969), also Peruvian.

Trotsky, born in the Ukraine of Jewish parents, was first inspired by the horrors of Czarism to support the Narodniks, a revolutionary peasant ideology, but soon became a Marxist and participated in the 1905 Russian Revolution. Despite early differences as a Menshevik opponent of the Bolsheviks, he became a close associate of Lenin. He led the Red Army during the 1917 Bolshevik Revolution and the subsequent Civil War (Deutscher 1954). After Lenin's death he lost out in the power struggles within the Communist Party and was exiled, eventually ending up in Mexico City. In 1940 he was murdered with an ice pick by Ramón Mercader on the orders of Stalin. He was a prolific writer and an important Marxist theorist.

Hugo Blanco, as a student in Argentina, became a Trotskyist. He notes that key concepts developed by Trotsky, including the notion of dual power, influenced his political work (Blanco 1977: 53). The concept of dual power was first developed by Lenin and further elaborated by Trotsky (Lenin 1964 [1917], Trotsky 2017 [1932]: 149). It argues that revolutions are clashes between different social classes. The construction of institutions, such as schools, courts and armed forces, alternative to those of the ruling-class state, is a necessary part of the process of liberation and transformation.

Trotsky's concept of permanent revolution, in turn, suggested that rather than being constrained to go through the same historical stages as more advanced capitalist countries had done, revolution in less developed states could be sustained and transformed into wider working-class revolution (Trotsky 2007).

In turn, he rejected Stalin's notion of socialism in one country to stress that revolution was international and ultimately global (Löwy 1981). Trotsky's monumental study *The History of the Russian Revolution* described in detail the process of revolution in a Russia with some similarities to Peru. Chapter Twenty entitled 'The Peasantry' articulates a Marxist view of agricultural labour and its potential for revolution, noting the danger that peasant demands for land would lead to a class of individualist wealthier peasants but observing nonetheless the revolutionary role of this social class:

> The subsoil of the revolution was the agrarian problem. In the antique land system, both directly out of serfdom, in the traditional power of the landlord, the close ties between landlord, local administration, and

caste zemstvo, lay the roots of the most barbarous features of Russian life, (Trotsky 2017 [1932]: 282).

In Peru, during the 1930s when Hugo was born, like Russia at the turn of the twentieth century, a large peasantry existed, along with a much smaller working class. The peasants were eager to break the power of the landlords and might do so, according to Marxists, by allying with workers.

Trotsky's main relevance for Hugo Blanco was the orthodox Marxist belief that the working class would be the agent of revolution, led by a strong revolutionary political party, with the peasants taking at best a supporting role. By the time of Hugo Blanco's entry into Marxist politics in the 1950s, the orthodox communist parties who followed Stalin seemed a somewhat conservative force in Latin America. Stalin's concept was that national liberation by an emerging middle class provided a stage towards communism, so for the time being he argued Marxists should support this. Trotsky's concept of combined and uneven development, the existence of both capitalism and underdevelopment, together with the dynamism of permanent revolution, seemed to suggest a more confrontational approach. As we shall see, Hugo was attracted to the Trotskyist rather than the Stalinist variety of Marxism.

Such dynamism was also expressed by a Peruvian Marxist who shaped Hugo's thinking, José Carlos Mariátegui. Both Mariátegui and Trotsky have a contradictory pull; in many ways promoting a communist orthodoxy based on Marx and Lenin, they also signal differences and complications. Both, of course, along with Lenin, stress that rather than promoting a view of inevitable, even mechanical, revolution, human action guided by examination of a particular context is necessary to bring social transformation.

Mariátegui was an innovative Marxist thinker who analysed the situation of Peru; concluding that the indigenous people were exploited, he noted their thirst for land reform. Mariátegui argued that Latin American Marxists could not simply borrow from Marx, Engels, Lenin and other European communists but had to be innovative, creating a distinct Marxism for their region. He drew strongly on indigenous culture and concepts, for example, the magazine he edited was entitled *Amauta*, which in Quechua means 'master or wise one' and is derived from the Incas.

His best-known work is *Seven Interpretive Essays on Peruvian Reality*. Mariátegui was injured as a child, his health remained poor and he died at the age of only 36. He travelled to Europe and was influenced by the well-known Italian Marxist Antonio Gramsci. In Peru he first worked politically with Haya de la Torre, who set up the left-wing but nationalist, and non-Marxist, APRA party. Disillusioned with de la Torre, Mariátegui founded the Socialist Party and became its first general secretary. It later became the Peruvian Communist Party. He also helped establish the General Confederation of Peruvian Workers (CGTP) (Vanden and Becker 2011: 17).

He viewed the collectivist nature of the Inca Empire, despite its undemocratic character, as an inspiration for the creation of communism in Peru. He examined the oppression of the peasants as a product of colonialism that had established a basically exploitative feudal system. Hugo Blanco read Mariátegui; a figure who links his interest in Marxism and indigeneity (Blanco 1977: 133). In this he was not unusual, much of the Marxist left in Peru have seen Mariátegui as an inspiration and most left groups in the country claim to be continuing his work.

José María Arguedas was from a Spanish speaking family but became a passionate supporter of all things indigenous. After his mother died in 1914 and his father remarried, he was largely brought up by indigenous servants, so at an early age became fluent in Quechua (Lambright 2010: 11). His passion for all things indigenous inspired him to become an anthropologist, and he catalogued Andean music, myths and other elements of culture. As a novelist and poet, he wrote in both Quechua and Spanish. Unlike other novelists who advocated indigenist ideas, who were predominantly white, his work showed the complexity of indigenous culture, rather than romanticising and simplifying it.

Arguedas' prose sometimes seems to describe Hugo's life and struggles; he was a keen chronicler of the struggle, in novels like *Todas las sangres* (All the Bloods), between peasant (*campesino*) and landlord (*gamonal*) in the Andes. He became active in the Communist Party while at university in Lima and was arrested and imprisoned in El Sexto jail. He has been described as a hybrid intellectual, both indigenous and European, living and writing about at least two worlds.

He exchanged letters with Hugo Blanco when Hugo was in prison. Deeply traumatised by his difficult childhood, he eventually committed suicide in 1969. While immersing himself in Quechua culture, he 'did not limit himself to strictly indigenous themes' but highlighted 'the marginal on many levels' (Lambright 2010: 16). His experience of hybridity was similar, as we shall see, to Hugo's; both spoke Quechua, both respected indigenous perspectives as just as rich and intellectually strong, if not more so, than those derived from Europe. He wrote in detail about the kinds of land struggles and the complexities of rural life in the Andes that Hugo was to experience.

Anthropology and literature were Arguedas' focus, but this was a political focus; he was aware of the macro power struggles of imperialism and capitalism and their manifestations at a local, micro level, down to conflicted family relations. It would be an oversimplification to see the Nobel Prize winning Peruvian novelist Mario Vargas Llosa merely as his antithesis; nonetheless where Llosa looks to modernity, Europe and capitalism, Arguedas champions indigeneity, rejecting capitalism and crude notions of linear progress (Morañ 2016). In *We the Indians*, Hugo challenged Llosa's critique of Arguedas (Blanco 2018a).

Hugo Blanco referred to Arguedas as his *tayta*, a Quechua word meaning 'father', used to show respect for an elder. While some might talk of the two Hugo Blancos, the Trotskyist and the indigenist, Hugo's affection for Arguedas shows that his thinking was strongly influenced by indigenous concerns during the 1950s and 1960s when he was most engaged with Trotskyism (Blanco 1977: 130). Indigenous is defined not in racial but social and cultural terms; Hugo noted that Arguedas had *indio sonqo,* an Indian heart. An examination of Arguedas' work suggests that the separation and interconnection between the 'white', the 'indigenous' and the mestizos or mixed was 'due to the language one speaks, the ancestry one recognizes, and the cultural tradition with which one identifies' (Lambright 2010: 262).

Hugo observed that the term 'Indian' was used in a derogatory way but could be reclaimed as a term (Blanco 2018a). Arguedas spoke of the resistance of the indigenous and looked to a day when they would rise and transform Peru. Both Arguedas and Hugo Blanco valued the culture of ponchos and other forms of indigenous dress, their myths and the *huaynos*, songs based on folklore traditions, full of metaphors and allusions. We will return to the significance of Hugo and Arguedas' views on language and its role in political struggle later.

Arguedas, Trotsky and Mariátegui were observers and advocates of political struggle. Rather than discussing utopian alternatives or pure principles, they were interested in how the oppressed could fight back against the rich and the powerful. Arguedas is remembered as a novelist and anthropologist but equally he was a political thinker of some sophistication, putting those at the margins at the centre of his novels and portraying insurrection. He has been theorised as a post-colonial advocate of revolutionary transformation:

This ultimate political moment occurs at the end of *Todos las sangres*: when the negotiation fails, the soldiers, representatives of the state, shoot Rendón Willka, and the indigenous communities all over the sierra rise in general rebellion, *yawar mayu*. (Feldman 2014: 9)

## Peru in context

It is impossible to understand Hugo Blanco without understanding a little about Peru. Peru is unique but with its violent colonial history, racist present and economy based on extractivist exploitation, it also shares features with much of our planet. Peru contains a number of distinct environments. In the east the *selva* exists, with the country blending into the vast Amazon rainforest. The *sierra*, consisting of the Andes mountains, runs through the centre, while the capital city of Lima is found on the flatter coastal area. The country is bordered by Ecuador to the north, Brazil to the east, Chile and Bolivia to the south (Hunefeldt 2004).

All nations are, as Benedict Anderson (1983) puts it, 'imagined communities'. Peru has not always been a political unit but is the product of relatively recent events based on rather violent dreams. The Spanish conquest destroyed what is commonly termed the Inca Empire but in Quechua is known as *Tawantinsuyu*, meaning the four '*suyu's* or regions. The area now called Peru has a rich history of highly organised political communities of which the *Tawantinsuyu* was merely the latest. The rich intellectual, cultural and organisational diversity was destroyed by the Spanish invasion. Incidentally, the word 'Inka' means ruler, but it was misused by the Spanish to describe the whole society and often spelt 'Inca'. *Tawantinsuyu* society apparently existed from around the thirteenth century AD until its destruction in the sixteenth (Pärssinen 1992).

Many early complex societies existed, the earliest so far discovered · by archaeologists is the Caral–Supe civilization found in Norte Chico in Northern Peru. Dating from around 3,500 BC this is the oldest known civilisation in the Americas, it contained cities, pyramids and sophisticated systems of irrigation canals (Shady *et al* 2001). Varied but equally complex societies existed at different points in what is now Peru. *Tawantinsuyu* society, organised as a single territory with a solar religious cult, standing army, and the Inca (sic) ruler borrowed a number of practices from pre-existing societies. Variously defined as a feudal, slave or socialist (either in a positive sense or from a totalitarian understanding) society, *Tawantinsuyu* constructed impressive buildings and roads and sustained a strong economy without markets or money. Because of this, it has remained a source of fascination for Peruvian Marxists, most notably Mariátegui. Other nations were incorporated into its expanding territories, either via negotiation or conquest. For example, the Chachapoyas of the Amazon were conquered just prior to the Spanish invasion. While we have no knowledge of their self-description, Chachapoyas means 'warriors of the cloud forest' in Quechua (Muscutt 1999). Tainted by its brutalities, *Tawantinsuyu's* sophistication should not be dismissed, and its cruelties were more than equalled by the European invaders who destroyed it, motivated by greed for its precious metals.

Francisco Pizarro (1471-1541), a Spanish soldier, arrived in Northern Peru with 180 followers in 1532. He marched on the city of Cajamarca, where Atahualpa 'the emperor was enjoying nearby mineral baths' (Werlich 1979: 39) Pizarro captured Atahualpa, who despite providing a ransom of enough gold and silver to fill two rooms, was murdered. Pizarro installed a puppet emperor and proceeded to loot the *Tawantinsuyu* territory. The invaders, despite their tiny numbers, had horses, guns and metal, all unknown to the society they met, so victory was relatively easy, despite the military power of *Tawantinsuyu*, which at the time controlled a huge territory from Ecuador to Chile. Pizarro was later killed by other Spanish invaders.

The Spanish monarchy appointed a governor to what was termed Peru, which may be derived from a mistranslation of a local name 'Biru'. Indigenous resistance occurred with a new *Tawantinsuyu* neo-Inca society created north of Cusco. In 1572 the Spanish destroyed this and executed the last Inca, Túpac Amaru. The indigenous population were essentially enslaved, and many were sent to mine silver, the largest mining complex being on Potosi, 'an entire mountain of silver' which is now in Bolivia (Hunefeldt 2004: 60).

The continuing oppression of indigenous people, particularly in the form of forced labour, led to resistance, most notably when Túpac Amaru II led an uprising in 1780. Eventually defeated, the authorities attempted to execute him by dismemberment, attaching each of his limbs to a horse. This failed, but he was quartered, beheaded and his body burnt. The botched execution took place at the main plaza in Cusco, where Túpac Amaru had also been killed in a similar manner (Chambers and Chasteen 2010: 36-37).

While Spanish domination had its complexities and the society was diverse to some extent, the basic model involved brutal subjugation of both the indigenous and the Afro-Peruvians, who arrived as slaves, to extract as much mineral wealth as possible, particularly in the form of silver. The Quechua and Aymara speaking descendants of the *Tawantinsuyu* lived in conditions of continuing degradation.

While Peru was something of a royalist stronghold, Bolivar's war of independence, which swept the Spanish monarch out of Latin America, eventually led to the creation of a republic. The Argentine general José de San Martín declared Peruvian independence on 28 July 1821, but it took several more years before the royalists were defeated (Hunefeldt 2004: 101). Values of democracy and rights promoted by the American Revolution of 1775 and the French Revolution of 1789 brought few benefits to non-

Spanish speaking Peruvians. This was still an economy based on quasi-feudal exploitation. Peru was ruled from independence to the 1940s by a combination of caudillos, military strong men, and elected leaders (Werlich 1979).

Given Peru's complex and brutal history, demands to modernise and create a secure state have given rise to a variety of movements and parties calling for reform. These have had a contradictory relationship to the past; some have argued that pre-conquest culture should be drawn upon and celebrated, giving political and economic status to indigenous peoples. The urge to modernise has been used to suggest that pre-Spanish societies were inferior and that all Peruvians should be assimilated into one essentially European culture.

Perhaps the most significant, but far from successful, political party in Peru during the twentieth century has been APRA. Founded by Haya de la Torre in 1924, the *Alianza Popular Revolucionaria* (American Popular Revolutionary Alliance), was an organisation inspired by the Mexican Revolution, founded with the aim of uniting a diverse variety of left-wing Peruvian forces. De la Torre, who worked for a time with Mariátegui, never became President but his party grew and became a strong force in Peruvian politics. De la Torre rejected Marxism, after an early ideological flirtation, promoting a pan-Latin American nationalism, challenging US dominance in the region, while advocating modernity and progressive policies (Löwy 1992: lviii). His programme called for:

(1)    Action of the countries of Latin America against Yankee Imperialism.

(2)    The political unity of Latin America.

(3)    The nationalisation of land and industry.

(4)    The internationalisation of the Panama Canal.

(5)    The solidarity of all the oppressed people and classes of the world.
       (Werlich 1979: 181)

APRA argued that a Peruvian middle class could lead their revolution. De la Torre built a disciplined, and in some ways rather fanatical following, variously contesting elections and, at other times, supporting armed action. Conservative forces, including the military, have through much of the twentieth century seen APRA as a major threat and worked hard to keep it out of power. The immediate political context of the 1930s when Hugo Blanco was born can be understood partly in terms of this struggle between APRA and the Peruvian right. APRA equally was to move right during its history, and as we shall see, Hugo Blanco came into dramatic conflict with Alan Garcia, a Peruvian President, elected on an APRA ticket. By 1933, APRA had recently lost an election, been involved in armed action and was subsequently outlawed by President Sanchez Cerro. An army officer supported by a military junta, Cerro was shot through the heart by Abelardo Mendoza Leiva, a member of the then banned APRA, on 30 April 1933 (Werlich 1979: 200). Hugo Blanco was born the next year into a Peru marked by a legacy of colonialism and almost permanent conflict.

# 2

# Early Life 1934-1958

'We must keep on fighting for a world with room for many different worlds.'
Hugo Blanco (2008c)

Hugo Blanco was born 15 November 1934 in the Cusco region of Peru. While an early biographer, Victor Villanueva, described him as a 'typical provincial petty bourgeois', this seems a little unfair. Certainly from an early age he had a strong connection with indigenous people and radical political currents (Alexander 1973: 170).

His family members, especially his older brother and sister, had thrown themselves into resisting the dictatorial Peruvian government, and Hugo, while still at school, was swept along by a tide of youthful militancy. Later, as a student in Argentina, he became a Trotskyist and trade union activist. Returning to Cusco, he was involved in a massive demonstration against Richard Nixon (at the time US Vice-President). This chapter outlines Hugo Blanco's early years of militancy until 1958, when he moved to Chaupimayo, deep in the countryside, to become a peasant farmer and to join an increasingly radical movement for land rights and indigenous freedom.

## Learning about oppression in Huanoquite

Hugo was brought up in Huanoquite, a district south of Cusco, his parents, Miguel Angel Blanco and Victoria Galdos, were also from Cusco. Hugo's maternal grandfather Daniel had been a powerful landowner and mayor of Huanoquite (Seligmann 1995: 120). Hugo described his family background:

My father was a lawyer, and my mother was the daughter of a landowner. She had three Indios (Indians) working for her on the piece of hacienda (plantation) she inherited.

In spite of these two incomes, my family was actually poor. Naturally in Cuzco we were middle class; but compared to Lima, or the level of more advanced countries, we were very poor. I was surprised when I went to Argentina to discover that the standard of living I had as a factory worker there was much higher than I had ever known in Cuzco as the son of a lawyer (Blanco 1971a: 12)

Hugo's first political commitments were rooted in school and university agitation along with an early awareness of the oppression of the local Indian peasants. Hugo immersed himself in indigenous culture from an early age; living in Cuzco, the centre of the *Tawantinsuyu* system, he was fascinated by archaeology. He noted how as 'a young boy, I enjoyed acting in a play we presented in Quechua' (Blanco 1971a: 13). He also favoured indigenous music. He met many indigenous people who were his father's clients and observed that, time after time, they lost their cases within a legal system biased towards powerful landowners. The early shocking incident, noted by Eduardo Galeano, where the landlord Bartolomé Paz physically branded a peasant with a hot iron, seems to have been pivotal in Hugo's development (Blanco 1977: 94). His parents had heritage which was both white and indigenous, but importantly they could speak Quechua. Language was key to both identity and oppression, Hugo used Spanish at school but spoke some Quechua at home.

While his father defended indigenous people as a lawyer, his mother taught him radicalism from an early age,

My mom taught me to be generous; that is to say, she gave me the ABCs of revolution: don't think about yourself, nor about those that you find only millimetres away from you, instead think about all those who suffer and need encouragement (Blanco 1962: 8).

Indigenous people were certainly suffering in the 1930s and 1940s in Cusco, they were largely excluded from education, were thus illiterate, their land was often stolen, and their labour power exploited for little or no reward. In a racist system, while a minority of intellectuals of European descent praised Peru's indigenous culture and history, most liberals and 'progressives' felt that a homogenous, modern, Spanish-speaking Peru provided the way forward. Such a future offered no place for indigenous people unless they integrated; their culture replaced by that of modernity. Some politicians would reference the glories of Peru's *Tawantinsuyu* past and promise reform, but they generally did little or nothing when in power to help indigenous people. The local establishment in Cusco was largely racist and reactionary, with the police, the courts and the political system excluding indigenous people. In the countryside, the landowners (*gamonales*) with their huge estates (*haciendas*) exploited the indigenous peasants (*campesinos*) as unpaid labour in a neo-feudal economic and social system.

Arguedas' novels and short stories vividly described such oppression. In *The Pongo's Dream,* the *pongo,* an indigenous servant, dies and travels to the afterlife with his *gamonal* master. As Saint Francis greets them, the *pongo* fears that his oppression will continue for eternity. The Saint, noted for his solidarity with the oppressed and nature, orders a beautiful angel to coat the landlord in honey. In contrast, the *pongo* is met by an ageing angel with 'scabby feet', who proceeds to smear him in excrement from a discarded gasoline can. The *gamonal* insists that right is being done but is dismayed when both master and servant are commanded to lick each other for eternity (Starn 1999: 34). The indigenous peasants dreamed of the great reversal, when the world would be turned upside down and the oppressed restored to rulership over their oppressors. Those who receive shit will change places with those who drip with honey. The Inca will return and restore order and justice to the world.

Hugo became aware of indigenous oppression from his earliest years. He recalled, in a prison letter written in 1969 to José María Arguedas, meeting an indigenous woman in 'nineteen hundred and forty-something' in the San Jeronimo market in Cusco. She told him that the priest has insisted that an earth tremor during mass was God's punishment 'because the Indians of the *ayllu* rose up against the Dominican Fathers of the Patapata hacienda'. (Blanco 1977: 127). The Dominicans had taken land from the communal *ayllu,* even though the indigenous had legal titles proving their ownership. The indigenous set up a union to try to defend their commons from enclosure by the church, selecting Lorenzo Chamorro as their secretary-general. The Dominicans tried to bribe Lorenzo, and when this failed they ordered their thugs to shoot him. Despite receiving six bullet wounds, he survived and was taken to hospital. The priest told his congregation that Lorenzo was the devil and unless the devil died in hospital God would punish them. There was, of course, as Hugo noted in his letter to Arguedas, no prison for those who shot Indians like Lorenzo.

Despite the later growth of liberation theology in parts of Latin America, including Peru, and the writings in the past of religious leader who defended the indigenous like Bartolomé de las Casas, the Catholic Church was often an oppressive force, stealing land and seeking to deny indigenous culture. The indigenous women in San Jerónimo Market told Hugo that the priest had threatened them:

My children, the Lord has pardoned this town, but you are abusing His kindness, your wives continue to visit the house of the devil. A rain of fires is going to fall on San Jerónimo! (Blanco 1977: 128)

The women feared the rain of fire, so stopped visiting Chamorro's wife. Hugo was unafraid, and indeed seemed to have little attachment to the Catholic Church, so visited Chamorro on many occasions, noting 'When I was 10, I met an indigenous leader who told me of his story and his struggles' (Blanco 2008a: 18).

On one occasion Chamorro asked Hugo if he knew Picol Hill, telling him that it was on the road from Paruro and, while far away, might be seen from Cusco. The 'cavalry guards' were sent to take the land, but the land resisted them with the *p'ata kiskas* (cactus) scratching them and the very stones in the earth showing their hatred of the enclosers. The Indians were armed with slings; Chamorro said that these were like the slings of Túpac Amaru's soldiers and numerous other indigenous armies but instead of stones they contained dynamite (Blanco 1977: 128).

These early memories, recounted in prison letters in the 1960s, show continuity in Hugo Blanco's thought: a linked respect for the indigenous, the environment, the commons and, above, all resistance. He may have embraced Lenin and Trotsky as a student in Argentina, Marxists who put the working class rather than the peasants at the centre of their revolutionary hopes, but the indigenous were always in Hugo's heart.

## High school subversion

Education struggles were also linked to indigenous resistance. Hugo's father, brother and sister were all involved in university and school protests. He learnt from his family, and his first activism began at school. Interviewed by *The Militant*, a US Marxist newspaper, he noted that his father had been involved in university protests. Attendance for students was mandatory but this made it impossible for those who worked to join a university, thus the 'Peruvian oligarchy attempted to make college education a class privilege'. (Blanco 1975a: 13). It was difficult for *campesinos* to take time off during harvests and other important points in the agricultural cycle to study. The demand to make university attendance more flexible was a demand for indigenous rights and freedom.

Hugo's older brother and sister were politically active. He described his older brother Oscar as an 'Indianista' and Aprista active in student protests (Blanco 1971a: 13). General Manuel Odría (1896 – 1974) took power in a coup in 1948, governing until 1956, a period termed the 'Ochenio'. He introduced a 'harshly authoritarian regime', which proclaimed a state of emergency and suppressed civil rights (Werlich 1979: 248). At this time supporters of APRA were strongly persecuted. Despite his own student experience of oppression, their father was opposed to Oscar and his sister Luchy's activism against the Odría regime. Hugo noted, 'For that reason their political activity was doubly underground: in the face of the capitalist state, and in the face of family repression' (Blanco 1975a: 13).

Because of his siblings' political involvement, the secret police raided the Blanco home, searching every room and interrogating family members. Hugo learnt to conceal items that might be incriminating and took care when visiting Oscar in his hiding place to avoid police surveillance. When Oscar was imprisoned at the age of seventeen, Hugo, then thirteen, became much more actively involved in supporting him. He would take food to Oscar in prison and smuggle out messages to Oscar's comrades. Hugo learnt how to work a mimeograph machine (generally called a duplicator in Britain). In the days before the internet and photocopiers, this was a means of producing propaganda such as simple leaflets and posters. Hugo noted that the imprisonment of his brother was a massive embarrassment to his family, and the jailing of his sister was an unimaginable tragedy. Both were freed, and Oscar later left the country (Blanco 1975a: 13).

Hugo, aged seventeen, attended the Colegio Nacional de Ciencias y Artes in Cusco, at the time the only publicly funded high school in the city. Hugo suggested that the college was known for its rebellious spirit and in 1951, when Peru's military government imposed an authoritarian principal, he and his fellow students went on strike. This was, apparently, both well organised, with delegates elected in each class, and 'well publicised by clandestine methods' (Blanco 1975a: 13). The strike was successful. He recounted how a negotiator was brought in to mediate between the striking students and their authoritarian principal,

> the students of all grades (from twelve to nineteen years old, more or less) were then awaiting him in parade uniform and perfect formation, but we refused to enter the school building so long as the principal was not replaced. The education ministry understood that it had to give in and removed him (Blanco 1975a: 13).

Another act of high school subversion occurred as part of the annual school band parade. Each year the school band would march as part of a high school parade, but in 1951 they were banned from doing so and had to march with the army band instead. On the day, they formed up next to the army band but marched to their own beat embarrassing the authorities again. The people watching applauded the high school students (Blanco 1975a: 14).

University students would strike and occupy, high school students would protest in solidarity with them and, in turn, younger pupils would support those in high school. The demand for flexible university attendance, won by the previous generation including Hugo's father, was annulled by the junta. The reinstatement of this right and calls for the removal of Dulante, the military imposed rector of Peru's largest university, were key demands in the early 1950s. Hugo was attending night school and coordinating strikes. The authorities suspended high school to pre-empt further strikes and the conflict took to the streets with swiftly organised meetings and demonstrations. The Workers' Federation of Cusco (FTC) went on strike to support the students, and action ended with the suicide of Dulante. During a university occupation in Cusco, a mounted policeman struck Hugo on his head and back with a sabre. Later, on the same protest, a tear-gas canister exploded next to him, causing him to faint and removing skin from his face (Blanco 1975a: 14).

His ideological loyalties were loose:

> I considered myself a socialist, a communist, Aprista, Indianista, an anti-imperialist, etc., all mixed up. The only Marxist book I ran across was one by Plekhanov, I think I understood two or three pages (Blanco 1971a: 13).

He and other students published leaflets in the name of APRA but had no official involvement with the party. During his early years of school student activism, he was sympathetic to both the Communist Party and APRA, both of whom he saw as persecuted and thus revolutionary groups. Political parties, even on the left, seemed reluctant to recruit school students, rejecting them as too young in Peru during the 1940s and 1950s.

## Argentina and the Fourth International

Hugo was soon to become a follower of Trotsky's Fourth International but in 1952, although he had heard of the Revolutionary Workers Party (POR), a Peruvian Trotskyist party, he had not actually met any of their members. Trotskyism was relatively weak in most Latin American countries apart from Bolivia and Argentina. Hugo was to become a member of POR's equivalent in Argentina, when he moved to the country to study agricultural science.

Argentina, even more so than Peru, witnessed dramatic political events during the 1950s. A coup removed President Juan Perón from power in September 1955. Perónism was a complex, contradictory political movement that drew both from the left, providing reforms for workers, and the right, with its cult of personality and support for fascist movements. Eva Perón, Juan's wife, who died in 1952, was an iconic figure who haunted the imagination of Argentinians. Shortly before her death she proclaimed in one of her typically melodramatic speeches, 'I will come again, and I will be millions' (Fraser and Navarro 1997: 193.) While Peru has not been short of contradictory political movements and ideologies, and Argentina too has an indigenous population in the form of the Mapuche, the political context was different. Perónism was neither negatively nor positively an important influence on Hugo Blanco's ideological development. However, his introduction to Trotskyism, during a rally against the 1954 coup in Guatemala, was to shape his thinking and inform his ever more radical commitments.

Hugo noted that he chose to study agronomy in Argentina because he liked farm work and his brother was already studying the course at University of La Plata in Buenos Aires Province:

I lived together with my brother Oscar who was General Secretary of the cell in La Plata, of APRA (American Revolutionary Popular Alliance – which was a leftist party in Peru that, like all the left, was persecuted in Peru by the dictatorship of Odría). Our room was practically the premises of APRA in La Plata. The exiled Apristas came to our room. I questioned them avidly about APRA politics. As APRA began to move right, I became disillusioned. Another party on the left was the Communist Party (pro Moscow); my brother took it upon himself to disenchant me by about them, showing me evidence of their defeatist attitudes that I could not refute. (Interview July 2018).

1954 was the year that the Guatemalan President Jacobo Árbenz was overthrown in a CIA backed coup. Guatemala in Central America, like Peru, had a huge oppressed indigenous population and had suffered from autocratic military rule. Like Peru, land was a vital issue within a largely peasant-based society. Elected on a moderate socialist manifesto, Árbenz had attempted to introduce land reform. This upset both the large landowners and the US based United Fruit Company; the CIA helped organise a military coup and thousands of citizens, particularly indigenous people, were killed (Schlesinger and Kinzer 1983).

The coup was to have a decisive effect on one young Argentine leftist, Ernesto Guevara, better known simply as 'Che'. To Che, who was living in Guatemala during the coup, the overthrow of a democratic socialist government suggested that non-violent electoral politics would achieve little or nothing. A revolution that did not go all the way would be crushed by the US state and domestic elites (Gott 1973: 64). He turned to guerrilla warfare and became one of the main figures leading the 1959 Cuban revolution. While the Cuban example was to have impact on Hugo in diverse ways, the rally against the coup in Guatemala was to have a significant influence on his political life. Perhaps if he had chosen to study that day, instead of going to protest, his life might have been very different?

Several of the speakers at the rally, including those from the Communist Party, argued that it was necessary to support a cross-class alliance of Guatemalan workers, peasants and the middle class to reverse the coup. In contrast, another speaker rejected such cooperation, instead 'insisting that the only way to protect Guatemala's political revolution was to arm the masses.' (Heilman 2000: 43). Overhearing friends complaining about a Trotskyist being allowed to speak, Hugo decided that he would become a Trotskyist too.

A central figure for Argentina Trotskyism was Nahuel Moreno (1924-1987) who was to have a deep influence on Hugo Blanco. Trotskyism was under constant threat, perhaps far more so than other left currents. Stalin waged a war against Trotsky and had him assassinated in Mexico in 1940. Trotskyists were under pressure and often used pseudonyms to hide their identity. Moreno's given name was in Hugo Miguel Bressano Capacete. 'Moreno' is Spanish for brown, and Brown's first name 'Nahuel' was derived from the Mapuche word for tiger. Moreno was converted to Trotskyism by a sailor and became an active militant:

> In 1944 Moreno founded his own group, the *Grupo Obrero Marxista* (GOM - Marxist Workers Group), which focused its activities on the workers' movement. Its efforts were directed to an area with one of the highest concentrations of workers in Argentina, the southern area of Greater Buenos Aires, and Avellaneda in particular. In January 1945, the GOM took part in the strike of 15,000 workers at the Anglo–Ciabasa meatpacking plant. Advised by Mateo Fossa (the leader of the timber workers' union who had interviewed Trotsky), they came to the strike with money they collected for the strike fund and offered their support. The strike was defeated. But this experience allowed them to preside over the *Club de Corazones Unidos* (United Hearts Club), a sporting and cultural club in the working class neighborhood of Villa Pobladora. (Liszt 2018)

When Hugo Blanco arrived in Argentina, the Grupo had grown and was known for publishing the newspaper *Palabra Obrera* (PO), Workers Word. Like most other Marxists, supporters of *Palabra Obrera* argued that the working class were the key agents of revolution and, as noted above, focused on trade union activity. It was significant too that Nahuel Moreno worked at the University of La Plata where Hugo studied. Hugo realised that he had a choice to make:

> I left the university and went to work in a factory, because I understood due to the *latifundismo* that reigned supreme at the time in Peru, my options as an agronomist would be to serve a landowner or even become one. (Blanco 2018a: 14)

Discussing this in 2018 he noted:

> I met a Peruvian Trotskyist exile who linked me to Argentine Trotskyists whose party was the POR (*Partido Obrero Revolucionario*). The main leader of that party was Nahuel Moreno. The POR was a member of the Fourth International (Trotskyist). I joined and played in that game. As I learned that for Marxism 'The proletariat is the vanguard class', I left the university and went to work as a worker in a cold storage unit where only temporary workers were accepted and then dismissed. (Interview August 2018)

So, Hugo Blanco left university, never to return, and became a worker at the Swift meat packing factory in Berisso, processing the beef from Argentina's vast population of cattle. He joined the plant's trade union and developed a strong friendship with Eduardo Creus, a seasoned Trotskyist militant who worked in a *frigorífico* (cold storage unit). Hugo described this as a hugely rewarding time of his life noting 'This was the best experience I have had participating in a revolutionary party in mass struggle' (Blanco 1975a: 14). The 1955 coup against Perón saw most students supporting the US backed and anti-trade union right. Hugo and his fellow workers resisted the right-wing forces. The new regime was described as '*gorilla*', a reference not to the great and intelligent ape, but derived from '*guerre*' the Spanish word for war, in reference to its militarist nature. By the 1970s similar *gorilla* regimes, headed by military dictators and supported by the US, governed much of Latin America.

The group around *Palabra Obrera*, while a disciplined Leninist organisation, highly active in working-class struggle, had little or no involvement with agricultural workers including indigenous people. Indeed, Trotsky saw the peasantry as allies in revolutionary struggle but put workers at the centre of his strategy for revolutionary social change. Marx and Engels, in turn, whom Lenin and Trotsky drew upon, also stressed the centrality of the organized working class in making revolution. Hugo Blanco noted, 'the Marxism of that time convinced me that the working class was the unquestionable vanguard' (Blanco 2018a: 14).

Three personalities dominated Latin American Trotskyism during the 1950s, as well as Moreno, Michel Pablo and Juan Posadas also deserve mention. While Trotskyism is sometimes described, fairly or not, as sectarian and divisive, with apparent personality differences and adherences to dogma being blamed, division was perhaps inevitable given the difficult political context. A straightforward adherence to a Leninist strategy was not always easy given the complex and shifting realities of both Latin America and the wider world in the 1950s.

In the 1950s, most Trotskyists were members of the Fourth International, established to be a world party of Marxist revolution in 1938, contrasted with the Third International created by Lenin but now representing Stalinism, and the earlier Second International which betrayed the workers by embracing the different sides in the First World War rather than rejecting the conflict as an imperialist war. But the Fourth International tended to split, to branch out and for the splintered branches to sometimes grow back together. Groups like the International Socialists (IS), whose British representative is the Socialist Workers Party, have rejected what they see as orthodox Trotskyism, to create new traditions based in part on Trotsky's writings but drawing on other Marxists such as Rosa Luxemburg, Max Shachtman or IS founder Tony Cliff (Kelly 2018).

A major split in the Fourth International occurred in 1953 with many national sections, including the supporters of PO in Argentina forming a faction in opposition to the political direction taken by Michel Pablo. While complex, these conflicts are relevant in understanding Hugo Blanco's political direction and the strategic challenges faced by the revolutionary left during this period. Pablo, the pseudonym of Michalis N. Raptis (1911–1996), was, along with Ernest Mandel, a leader of the Fourth International. Backed by the US Socialist Workers Party, Pablo had played an important role in uniting the International and shaping its strategic direction, but in 1951 the new perspective he was advancing for the organisation caused bitter dissent. Pablo noted the dominance of official Communist Parties, the relative weaknesses of the Trotskyists, and the likelihood of World War Three occurring (Camejo 2010: 116). He believed that war would help strengthen dissent within Communist Parties and that the Fourth International should prepare to exploit this.

Given these assumptions he advocated deep entry with members of the Fourth International secretly joining Communist Parties or social democratic parties as a long-term project to exploit the subsequent divisions caused by likely war. While this might be seen as an imaginative way of leveraging power for a relatively small political organisation, it was perceived understandably by many Trotskyists as scandalous. Given that Stalinists had killed Trotsky, how was it justifiable or indeed practical to join Stalinist political parties? Pablo was widely condemned as a liquidationist crypto-Stalinist.

Moreno's *Palabra Obrera* network, along with many other Trotskyite groups across the planet, formed an International Committee of the Fourth International (ICFI) as a rival to the Fourth International led by Pablo. Pablo's influence waned and he was eventually ousted. The Fourth International and ICFI reunited in 1963. Pablo's subsequent political direction was innovative and radical; he was already a passionate supporter of anti-colonial liberation struggles in Asia, Africa and Latin America. This contrasted with the accepted Marxist orthodoxy that the revolution would be centred on the most advanced industrial countries such as Britain, the US and Germany.

In 1961, Pablo participated in the Algerian independence struggle against France. He also became an advocate of workers' self-management, suggesting a more decentralist and libertarian form of Marxism. Pablo also supported feminism. Most strikingly with his supporters in the tiny International Revolutionary Marxist Tendency, during the 1970s, he promoted ecological politics (Greenland 1998). One Australian supporter of Pablo, the physicist Alan Roberts, wrote an early account of such a red green synthesis entitled *The Self-Managing Environment* (Roberts 1979). The 1970s, though, provided a very different political context from the 1950s, when Hugo Blanco became a Trotskyist.

Juan Posadas, pseudonym of Homero Rómulo Cristalli Frasnelli (1912–1981), was like Moreno an Argentine born Trotskyist. He headed the Latin American Bureau of the Fourth International and had some success in strengthening the movement during the 1940s. In 1953, he took the side of Pablo, leaving those supporting the International Committee of the Fourth International (ICFI) in a weak position in several countries, as many Trotskyists in Latin America took his and Pablo's side rather than that of Moreno and the rest of the ICFI. Later ridiculed for writing about the socialist civilisation of aliens; after all, Posadas argued, only socialism would raise the productive forces necessary for interplanetary travel, he was during the 1950s very much a traditional Marxist. While not central to Hugo's political development Posadas was, of course, a well-known figure in Latin American Trotskyism for many years (John 2009: 179).

## Trade unionism and Trotskyism in Peru

Writing in 1975, Hugo rather modestly noted that in 1957 he had gone back to Peru, 'worked in some factories' and organized a small Trotskyist group. He was active in Lima, Peru's capital city (Blanco 1975a: 14). The PO network in Argentina asked Hugo Blanco to return to Peru to help 'reconstruct the Peruvian section of the Fourth International'. He lived with two comrades and found a job at a factory. His aim was to get involved in trade union activism at the factory, but to join the factory union, six months of good behaviour was necessary (Interview July 2018).

The Peruvian Trotskyist *Partido Obrero Revolucionario* (POR) split into two, both using the same name. The majority group supported Pablo and Posadas, while the smaller group that Hugo joined stuck with Moreno and the ICFI. Not only were the Moren- aligned POR a splinter, but Trotskyists were widely distrusted on the Peruvian left. Héctor Béjar, a Peruvian revolutionary and guerrilla, writing in the 1960s, observed:

Hugo Blanco was and is a disciplined Trotskyist militant. This fact posed a serious problem for the Left. Hadn't it been said for many years that the Trotskyists were imperialist agents? Hadn't Trotskyism been characterised repeatedly as a counter-revolutionary tendency? The years of Stalinism were not far off, no one had withdrawn the supreme anathema against Trotskyism. It continued in full force. (Béjar 1970: 53)

Trotskyism in Peru may have been inspired by contacts in Bolivia, a country where a mass Trotskyist movement has been significant (John 2009). The Peruvian POR that Hugo had joined originated in a group created in 1944 by textile workers, who had left the Communist Party because they felt it had betrayed them in a strike. They, along with a small number of intellectuals, published a paper entitled *Cara y Sello* (Façade and Reality) and they called their group *Grupo Obrero Marxista* (GOM). A new paper entitled simply *Revolución* was published and they became the POR in 1947. They gained some publicity in 1953, when the Odría regime accused them, along with their rivals in the much larger Peruvian Communist Party, of leading a strike the southern city of Arequipa (Alexander 1973). Hugo was aware of their repression by the authorities but knew little about them, assuming wrongly that they were supporters of Stalin's Soviet Union, which 'I was beginning to realise was quite conservative' (Blanco 1971a: 13).

The POR produced a manifesto that quoted Mariátegui and unsurprisingly advocated a revolutionary strategy based on the 1917 Bolshevik model, involving the creation of joint committees of workers, peasants and soldiers.

The workers would create a dictatorship of the proletariat with the support of peasants (Alexander 1973: 157-159). Despite this ambition they remained a small group and, as noted, split in two during the 1950s.

Hugo, along with the Moreno sympathising POR and much of the rest of the Peruvian left, were involved in the May 1958 demonstration against Richard Nixon. American foreign policy was becoming more unpopular in Peru, partly no doubt because of the CIA backed coups in Guatemala (1954) and Argentina (1955) but also because US tariffs had been placed on some Peruvian exports:

Nixon expressed a desire to visit San Marcos University and explain his government's policy to student critics. However, the Peruvian Student Federation issued a statement, replete with Marxist jargon, declaring that the North American emissary would not be welcome on their campus. Peruvian officials and the United States embassy urged Nixon to stay away from the school. But the vice-president asserted to avoid San Marcos would give a victory to the Communists, whom he seemed certain were behind the recent surge in anti-Americanism. A large hostile crowd met Nixon's motorcade at the entrance of the university. For a time, the students merely directed angry questions concerning mineral tariffs at the Yankee visitor. Then the throng began to hiss, shout, and throw stones, forcing the Nixon party to make a hurried retreat. (Werlich 1979: 264)

The government of Manuel Prado, elected in 1956, was incensed at the rough reception Nixon received and launched a wave of repression, forcing Hugo, who had helped organise the protest, to leave his factory job and get out of Lima (Blanco 1975a: 14). He had not been working at the factory long enough to have even joined the union. The POR were keen for him to avoid arrest and wanted him to become involved in a wave of strikes and protests that were growing in Cusco, where he had grown up (Heilman 2000: 45).

There I found that my sister worked as a journalist in a newspaper. The newspapers were not sold in kiosks, they were sold by children (called *canillas* or *canillitas*) shouting through the streets. I considered that they were oppressed and organized them. (Interview July 2018)

Hugo helped the newspaper sellers, aged between eight and nineteen years old, to create the impressively named Amalgamated Union of Newspaper Retailers. Because of their strike action and the help he gave them, he was briefly imprisoned (Heilman 2000: 45).

Hugo Blanco's activism as a member of the minority Moreno aligned POR was modest, imaginative and effective. Seeking to organise workers in the city of Cusco, 1958 saw him move to the countryside to start aiding the peasants in a struggle for land and freedom. Jaymie Heilman in her account of Hugo's early life, entitled 'Leader and Led: Hugo Blanco, La Convención Peasants, and the Relationships of Revolution', argues that while Hugo was looking to act as an organiser, promoting revolutionary militancy, the peasants of La Convención were looking for a skilled activist, able to speak Spanish and experienced legally and politically, to further their struggles.

Although Hugo was to become the public iconic face of a peasant uprising, the peasants had been patiently organising for many years to challenge the neo-feudal and racist order in which they lived. Trotskyists like Nahuel Moreno were becoming increasingly aware too of the importance of the struggle of the peasants for land reform and political rights. While Argentina was noted for its workers struggles, building on the insights of Mariátegui, Moreno argued:

> If it is true that the purposes of the European colonization were capitalist and not feudal, the colonists did not establish a capitalist system of production because there was no army of free labor on the market in America. Thus the colonists, to exploit America in a capitalist manner, were obliged to call upon non-capitalist productive relations: slavery or the semi-slavery of the indigenous people. (Moreno quoted in Löwy 1992: xl)

Hugo realised that the Cusco peasants were the 'vanguard of the struggle in the region' (Blanco 2018a: 14). His involvement with their campaign occurred because of a chance encounter. Hugo was arrested and held by the police on several occasions, at least once at the instigation of a newspaper owner.

> To my surprise, I met Andrés Gonzales, who was a leader of the Chaupimayo union of La Convención, whom I had seen at the Cusco union assemblies.
>
> He told me, 'Since you are not imprisoned by order of the judge, according to the law, you cannot be detained for more than 24 hours. On the other hand, they are going to send me to prison to await the trial that the landowner Romainville has initiated for us. It worries me a lot, because we have three leaders, including me in prison and as the

landowner is terrible, the comrades may be intimidated and stop fighting.'
I told him: 'I'm going to Chaupimayo so that doesn't happen.' (Interview
July 2018)

Hugo visited the other imprisoned campesino leaders. Óscar Quiñones
and Constantino Castillo agreed with Gonzales that Hugo should go to
Chaupimayo. They spoke with a friend who had come to visit them in
prison and asked him to find a horse so that Hugo could ride from the
nearest train station.

Andres Gonzales took on Hugo as a sub-tenant. The indigenous rented
small plots from the landowning Spanish-speaking elite and, in turn, some
could sublet to tenants. The three *campesino* leaders knew that Hugo's move
to the countryside meant that he could aid the peasants in their struggle.
He noted, 'I arrived on horseback at Chaupimayo, where they received me
well because I was sent by their imprisoned leaders,' adding, 'this was my
incorporation into the peasant movement'. (Interview August 2018).

During Hugo's life, he witnessed or was associated with many key
episodes in Latin American political history, thus his story is also the story
of the diverse Latin American left from the 1950s to twenty-first century. In
his early years, as has been noted in this chapter, he observed the indigenous
struggles rooted in Peru's history, gave solidarity to his Aprista brother and
sister, became a Trotskyist because of the Guatemalan coup in 1954 and lived
through the fall of Perón in Argentina. In turn, the turmoil of the Fourth
International, divided between supporters and opponents of Michel Pablo,
is part of his story. However, Hugo's arrival in La Convención meant that he
moved from observing and even participating in events, to making history.
Starting in the summer of 1958, he helped the peasants to rise, using strikes,
occupations, and eventually armed self-defence, to advance their cause. As
a result, he was to spend much of the 1960s in prison, but he certainly set
an example. The events of the La Convención uprising are the subject of
Chapter Three.

# 3
# Land or Death 1958-1963

'There is no victory without struggle'. Hugo Blanco (2011a)

In 1958 Hugo Blanco moved to La Convención to become a sub-tenant farmer, where he joined an on-going peasant campaign for land and rights. As the peasants were attacked by the land owners, their lackeys and the police, Hugo helped organise community self-defence. An uprising accelerated and the slogan *Tierra o muerte!* was heard not just in Cusco but across the whole of Peru. Despite Hugo's eventual capture, the uprising achieved its goal of land reform. This chapter will recount the best-known episode of Hugo Blanco's life during the years from 1958 to his capture in May 1963. Before doing so, the environmental, economic and social background will be introduced.

## La Convención

The peasant uprising in La Convención, between 1958 and 1964, captured the imagination of the world. Thousands of *campesinos* undertook strikes, mass protests and eventually occupations, against a basically feudal system. A contemporary report from Norman Gall, a British journalist, captures the sense of this militancy, reporting a mass meeting at the time:

> Several times a year on Saturday nights, the peasants of the Valley of La Convención at the eastern base of the Andes in southern Peru used to forgather in the sprawling. dusty plaza of this tiny market town. They would start coming around midnight, the men marching six abreast in sandals cut from old rubber tyres and shouting '*Tiara a muerte!* [*sic*]' – 'Land or death!' They carried no weapons, although the barefoot women who followed them, some with infants bound to their backs in shawls, had rocks bundled in their wine-colored homespun skirts. The men wore faded brown ponchos and floppy sheepskin hats. Their next day's lunch, pieces of yucca and salted meat, was tied inside sweat-stained sashes around their waists.

When dawn came, they formed small groups around the benches of the plaza, watched uneasily from the police station by Civil Guards. By noon, there were usually three thousand in the plaza for these political meetings of the peasant leagues, or *sindicatos*. They came on asses or in trucks from the remote haciendas of the Valley; many had traveled all night, sustained by the sugar-based brew called *aguardiente*. Through the afternoon they cheered in Spanish and Quechua (the Andean vernacular once used by the Incas) as their leaders urged them to seize the land 'because it is ours' and to stop providing labor on the haciendas. They cheered whatever they heard. (Gall 1967: 36)

The central demand of the uprising was summarised in the slogan *Tierra o Muerte!* meaning, of course, 'land or death'. This slogan, coined by Hugo Blanco with reference to Zapata's Mexican Revolution, misspelt by Norman Gall, acted as a rousing call to action. The indigenous people wanted land. If they had access to land, they could sustain their lives and live in dignity.

La Convención Valley, the centre point of the uprising, is approximately ninety miles north of the city of Cusco. La Convención was created as an administrative unit in 1857 but was a significant part of the *Tawantinsuyu* system; indeed it borders Machu Picchu, Peru's best-known tourist site. The historian Eric Hobsbawm, who visited in the 1960s, noted that its high mountains had cut if off from much of Peru during the nineteenth and earlier centuries. Indeed, its provincial capital Quillabamba wasn't built until the 1890s (Hobsbawm 1969: 33). It has connections with the high Andes and the Amazon, and can be seen as transitional between the two, socially, economically and ecologically.

The province of La Convención is environmentally diverse. The main action of this chapter occurred in the valleys, which were lower, wetter and warmer. While La Convención contains high mountains, they have been largely marginal for agricultural purposes. The area immediately below the mountains are *puna* i.e. grass covered plains where it rarely rains. Descending, the basic crop is potatoes, but *oca*, a tuber which is used as an alternative to potatoes, is also important, along with quinoa. As well as cattle and horses, llamas and alpacas, both camelids, are important species. Another camelid, the vicuña, incidentally the national animal of Peru and found on the country's coat of arms, also lives in this area. Hugo noted that while the vicuña was endangered, and in theory protected, the powerful landowners and civil guards often hunted them. Vicuña wool was illegally exported to the USA (Blanco 1977: 25). Descending further from the mountains down the valleys, temperatures rise but there is still little rain; in this zone, wheat is the staple crop along with the plants cultivated in the *puna*.

Hugo described the temperate valleys as the 'anteroom to the Amazonian rainforest' (Blanco 1977: 26). These valleys, transitional between the *sierra* (mountains) and *selva* (tropical forests), have been described colourfully as within the Ceja de la Montana, 'eyebrow of the mountain' (Craig 1969: 278). The valleys are known in Quechua as *yunka* meaning the inside and contrasted with the rest of the landscape which was described as the outside (Blanco 1977: 26).

Wesley Craig, a sociologist from Brigham Young University, carried out fieldwork in La Convención between September 1964 and May 1965. He outlined the history of ownership in the area. Intensively cultivated during the *Tawantinsuyu* period and before, *Tawantinsuyu* society used rock lined terraces on the valleys steep sides to grow coca leaves, which were transported using their famous rock cut roads (Craig 1969). Another stimulant dominated the twentieth century La Convención, with coffee becoming an increasingly significant cash crop. Indeed Hugo Blanco grew coffee on his small sublet piece of land.

The Spanish occupation of La Convención began in 1541 with the Huyro estate being transferred to the wife of Corregidor of the Audiencia of Cusco. This was just eight years after Pizarro conquered Cusco (Craig 1969: 278). Originally the land in the *sierra* was organised around the *ayllu*, a commons, where land was owned by the community. This form of ownership was exploited by the *Tawantinsuyu* system when they took control of the area, and the Spanish invaders, in turn, enclosed much of the land to create huge estates known as *haciendas*. Even after Latin American independence from Spain in the early nineteenth century, these huge estates owned by landowners, generally of European descent, continued to exist (Blanco 1977: 28).

These landowners had great difficulty in finding the labour they needed to farm their huge estates; the lush vegetation meant that the valley areas were both fertile and labour intensive. The indigenous, known as the Machiguenga, were reluctant to be enslaved as agricultural labour. Most of them either moved into the forests or were killed. By 1914, there were only about a thousand Machiguenga in La Convención (Hobsbawm 1969: 38). Converted to Christianity, they were forced to work when they came to the churches which were all on the land of major landowners. In early times, African slaves had been introduced to the region to work the land. Increasingly the *sierra* dwelling, Quechua speaking population were brought into the valleys to replace the earlier indigenous. Hugo Blanco noted that these people were 'transplants', used to a very different environment and agriculture, who had to work hard to make the valley land ready for cultivation (Blanco 1977: 27).

Interviewed in July 2018, Hugo described how Quechua speaking peasants, from higher altitudes, participated in,

> a system with feudal characteristics in which the landowner gave small plots to the indigenous peasants so that they could work for themselves. As payment for that plot they had to work without salary for the landowner. The haciendas of La Convención and the adjacent valley of Lares (in the province of Calca) was [...] a semi-tropical zone that produced plants of that climate (coffee, tea, cocoa, oranges, bananas, avocados, papayas, etc.). The area was inhabited with free Indians (Wachipairis, Machiguengas, Piros). These free Indians did not want to work for the hacendados, they preferred to retreat into the interior of the jungle. The hacendados were forced to recruit indigenous people from the sierra. It is difficult for an indigenous person, whether a commoner or a hacienda worker, to leave their homeland. They went to La Convención and Lares the boldest, knowing that the products of that area had a good price and they would earn more money. They had to get used to different type of food, the women had to change their warm woollen clothes for light clothes because of the heat (the *serranos* that went to the jungle brow, pale, sickly, were called *upichos*). The *haciendas* in La Convención and Lares were large, so the plots that they gave to the peasants were also larger than in the sierra, they called them 'leases' and the peasants were called *arrendires* and the days they had to work for the landowner was called a 'condition'. As the time was not enough to work the days of 'condition' for the landowner and their own crops, they took other mountain farmers, with whom they applied the same system as the landowners, gave them a small plot to work for themselves, and in payment for it they had to work a certain number of days in the crops of the '*arrendire*' or in those of the hacendado instead of the *arrendire*. In addition, there were peasants who entered the area seasonally to work for wages, they were called *habilitados*.

The various feudal dues or 'conditions' included unpaid construction of roads (*faena*), transport of crops and other farm products (*propio*) and domestic work in the landlord's households (*pong*). Pack animals could only be pastured by the peasants if they gave some of them to the *gamonales*; this was known as *yerbaje*. All of these duties meant days of unpaid work each month for the campesinos. They scratched a living on their own small plots and the most oppressed, the *pongos,* worked as servants, as in Arguedas's story *The Pongo's Dream* (Blanco 1977: 29).

So, in 1958, in a world of television, satellites and potential nuclear war, the peasants of La Convención were entangled in a social, economic and ecological system, that Hobsbawm described as 'neo-feudalism' (Hobsbawm 1969). It might be more accurate to drop the 'neo'; the peasants were living under a feudal system, but between 1958 and 1963 they organised, recruited Hugo Blanco to help with the task, rose up and smashed this system. If revolution is the destruction of a mode of production, in the sense of an economic system of ownership, over-determined by cultural, political and ecological factors, the La Convención uprising was indeed a revolution.

There is a vast academic controversy about how feudalism in a European sense can be defined and whether the concept is relevant outside of Europe. It is clear that a stratified society existed, with the peasants providing labour to a class of powerful landowners. Despite the views of critics such as Tom Brass (1989 and 2017), the notion of feudalism or neofeudalism put forward by Hobsbawm and other writers such as Villanueva (1967) describing La Convención seems realistic. Certainly as Hugo observed, this was a system with feudal characteristics.

## Campesinos and gamonales

When Hugo Blanco arrived in 1958, three different overlapping systems might be said to have coexisted in the valleys: 1) the remnants of the communal system of the *ayllu,* which had been greatly eroded and enclosed but existed still; 2) a creeping capitalist agricultural system; and 3) the feudalism of *gamonales.* However, the feudal system was dominant. Hobsbawm noted that by 1960 there were around 100 *haciendas* in La Convención and Lares. The largest, Huadquina, was part a five hundred-thousand-hectare estate acquired by Mariano Vargas in 1865. Huadquina was one of a number of *haciendas* owned by the dominant Romainville family. Much of the land was uncultivated because, as has been noted, the *gamonales* found it difficult to acquire the labour they needed to work the land (Hobsbawm 1969).

Within a global capitalist economy, commodity production and cash crops were infiltrating the region, with both the *gamonales* and *campesinos* sensing opportunities for commercial gain in the late 1950s. In 1928, the railway had reached Machu Picchu, and by 1933 a new road had been built to Quillabamba. Growth in investment and population was halted by an outbreak of malaria that lasted until the late 1940s. By the 1960s, increasing numbers of indigenous people from the neighbouring provinces of Urubamba, Calca, Anta, Acomayou and Apurimac, had moved to La

Convención, seeking a new life. Coffee prices and production rose sharply between 1945 and 1954 (Craig 1969: 283). Most *campesinos* found life tough at the end of the 1950s and their priority was to gain land, political rights and to end their unpaid obligations to the big landowners.

Hugo Neira, a journalist from Lima's *Expresso* newspaper, wrote a book entitled *Cuzco: Tierre y Muerte*, i.e. Cusco: Land and Death. He identified the grievances of the *campesinos* and summarised the context:

*Basic Problem*: Ownership of the land in the South.

*Departments*: Cuzco and Puno.

*Social Situation*: Out of 9 million hectares of arable land and natural pastures, 3 per cent of the owners possess 83 per cent of the farm area and 97 per cent of the owners posses 17 per cent of the remaining area

*Reason for the Conflict*: There is no adequate agrarian law and the peasants, organized in unions, oppose the tenant system, demanding ownership of the land.

*Additional*: They live in very bad conditions with a daily intake of less than 1,200 calories, comparable to a concentration camp. High infant mortality – smallpox, tuberculosis, whooping cough and dysentery. Three million exploited peasants at the margin of society.

*Maximum wage*: Eight soles [about $ .32] a day

(Neira translated by Maitan 1965: 38)

A number of other points should be made before moving back to the narrative of the La Convención uprising. First, as Hugo noted in *Land or Death*, there was a strongly racial element to the system. Indigenous people were oppressed by people of European descent. *Gamonales* tended to be whiter. While the earlier indigenous Machiguenga had been driven off, and perhaps the entire population was mixed to some extent, the language was very much a marker, with Quechua speakers discriminated against by those with a Spanish tongue.

In turn, many, although not all, *gamonales* acted with cruelty. Acts of physical punishment, humiliation, rape and other forms of sexual violence were common. The excesses of Alfredo Romainville from Chaupimayo were especially notorious. He once had a *campesino*, who had accidentally burnt part of a straw roof of a storage hut, hung from a mango tree and flogged for many hours. On another occasion a *campesino*, who apparently could not find a horse to take produce to market, was forced on to all fours and made to carry seventy kilos of coffee, while being whipped. Romainville denounced his own daughter, whose mother was a peasant, as a communist and had her jailed. Another land owner Márquez drowned his children, whose mother he had raped, in the local river (Blanco 1977: 94). At its worst the neofeudal system generated horrifying abuse. However the *campesinos* were increasingly organised and fighting back. It was certainly not the case, and is never claimed by Hugo, that he initiated the resistance; by the time of his arrival in 1958 the campesinos were already developing a combative and strong social movement.

## The roots of resistance

In 1958 Hugo Blanco became an *allegado in* Chaupimayo. Those indigenous who had access to small plots of land, were known as *arrendires*. They were keen to use their small parcels of land to grow coffee, exploiting the boom in prices. Their labour was restricted because of their obligations to the *gamonales*, so the sub-letting of their land to the *allegados*, was a way of taking advantage of the situation. A hierarchy with *gamonales* at the top and *allegados* at the bottom was apparent. The *arrendires* too were squeezed within a brutal system.

Hugo had married Vilma Valer Delgado during this period. Their daughter Carmen, who now lives in Sweden and is active in feminist and Latin American solidarity movements, was born in 1959:

> Vilma de Blanco [was] from Cusco. Hugo and Vilma´s brother Vladimiro were comrades and due to their friendship Hugo and Vilma met. At that time Vilma studied law. They got one daughter Carmen and when Hugo had to go to La Convención Vilma stayed in Cusco and they married for more social support from a conservative surrounding. They were married until [the] 1980s in spite of only a short cohabitation and many years of separation. (Comment from Gunilla Berglund August 2018)

Hugo's life was divided between the city and countryside, with activism continuing in the city of Cusco at this point. In 1959 he took part in a general strike called in response to President Prado raising the price of petrol. According to Hugo, the often-cautious Communist Party prevented the Workers' Federation of Cusco (FTC) from backing the strike. Nonetheless, strike committees formed, and pickets were organised. As usual Hugo was at the forefront of all this and as usual he was targeted by the authorities. As he was taking part in a picket, the police attempted to throw Hugo into one of their cars. Despite a police officer brandishing a gun, he resisted. The strikers responded by throwing rocks which broke the police windscreen, forcing Hugo's release. Well known to the authorities, he was later arrested, imprisoned and charged with 'attacking the armed forces' (Blanco 1975a: 14).

Imprisoned in Cusco in 1960, Hugo needed a defence campaign to gain his freedom. The FTC labelled Hugo and other supporters of the strike as provocateurs. As a *campesino* working in the countryside he was also a member of the *Sindicato de Campesinos de Chaupimayo* (SCCh). They were supportive but could not go on strike to demand his freedom, as they were already striking over another dispute. After two and half months of imprisonment, Hugo went on hunger strike to demand his freedom, the SCCh members also went on hunger strike in solidarity, and this in turn forced the FTC to act on his behalf. In response Hugo was released but had to report to the police once a week. This was challenging as he now lived some distance from Cusco city in an area with poor transport links:

> This was very hard for me since I worked and lived in the countryside. I had to go more than fifteen kilometres on foot through the mountains under a semitropical sun and then hope by chance a truck would pass by. And all this just so I could report to the nearest police headquarters. Then I had to do the same thing to get back. (Blanco 1975a: 14).

He eventually told the police that work commitments made it impossible to continue reporting and he never went back. This was in 1960, and Hugo was soon to enter the most dramatic phase of his life.

The *campesinos* were becoming both angry and better organised. Faced with abuse by the *gamonales* and little or no support from the official judicial system, they were already acting. On occasions *gamonales* were even killed; for example, on 28 August 1956, Alberto Duque of hacienda San Pedro was ambushed and executed by four *campesinos* whom he was attempting to evict (Heilman 2000: 28). Non-violent protests increased but were largely ignored, the authorities had little interest in rural communities, and where they did intervene they sided with the *gamonales*.

Trade union organisation was seen as a way of gaining strength to challenge abuse and improve and enforce contracts. The hacienda Huyro union was formed because the *gamonal*, his administrator and sons had 'exploited tenants, abused them, and raped peasant women and girls' (Heilman 2000: 28). One union member, Francisco Condori Huarca, explained their motivation:

> We thought about forming a union, we all entered into conversation, *arrendires* and *allegados* to form the union. Why? Because the *hacendado* exploited us, he did not pay us for our work, he threw us off our plots. [...] [he] exploited us like donkeys. (Heilman 2000: 28-29).

The process seems to have begun in 1947 when two *campesino*s at the Maranura *hacienda*, Justo del Pozo and Francisco Gamarra Loayza, formed a union and had success in gaining rights. The 1952 Bolivian revolution, when the population, including many indigenous *campesinos*, overthrew the government and occupied land, may have accelerated the process of union organisation in Peru. By 1958 there were fifteen unions in total in La Convención and Lares. They made demands for an end to physical abuse, an eight-hour working day, and to allow schools (Heilman 2000: 28). Alfredo Romainville, for example, had banned schools on his land and many other *gamonales* were hostile to the indigenous being educated.

Hugo Blanco noted that some *gamonales* were prepared to negotiate but many were appalled by the 'Indians having the impertinence to discuss how to serve the landlords.' At least two landlords were said to have been so shocked that they died of heart attacks (Blanco 1975a: 15). The authorities issued a ruling making it illegal for tenants to form a union, but this did little to halt unionisation. Alfredo Romainville was particularly incensed by the threat to his authority, taking legal action against nearly a hundred *campesinos,* many of whom he had imprisoned. This was how Andrés Gonzales, Leonides Carpio and Fortunato Vargas came to be imprisoned in Cusco city. As Hugo noted, the peasants of Romainville's Chaupimayo estate, who had lived through his tyrannical rule 'trembling with fear', became the vanguard of the struggle (Blanco 1975a: 15). Their militancy made the *gamonales* and indeed the authorities and elites across the whole of Peru tremble too.

As more estates were unionised, links between different estate unions grew and a province-wide network was gradually established. Union organisers tried to contact unions and leftist organisations in Cusco to gain help and, above all, practical advice on how to organise effectively. The FTC responded first with legal help and then by sending organisers into the region. With the aid of the FTC, the *campesinos* were able to file legal claims to try to enforce existing contracts and laws. With increased confidence and better organisation, a province-wide *campesino* union was created and more serious efforts were made to improve the conditions and erode the neofeudal system which the peasants found so oppressive. For example, the Maranura union went on strike until they won a reduction in their labour obligations and improved rights to their land. While the FTC was helpful to the *campesinos*, greater militancy was supported most strongly by Hugo Blanco, who threw himself into union organisation from the summer of 1958,

The union bought a used mimeograph, in which it produced flyers about the abuses of Romainville, whom we called 'the monster of La

Convención'.

In the FEPCACYL the colleagues from various unions asked me to visit them to produce leaflets about the abuses of the respective landowners. They gave me money for paper, ink and stencil paper that is used to print in mimeograph. I went to the next assembly with the printed flyers. Since the newspapers did not publish any of the outrages of the hacendados, the peasants were happy with these flyers. (Interview July 2018)

By 1961 the *campesino* union for the wider area had become a significant organisation. Hugo was elected as a delegate and a member of the executive committee, taking part in regular province-wide meetings in Cusco. However, Hugo's failure to attend the police headquarters in the city led to his arrest on the way to an executive meeting. Hugo insisted to the police that it was important for him to attend the meeting and that if allowed to do so he would report to the them the next day. Fearing mobilisation against them, the police agreed. Hugo attended the meeting and reported to the police in the morning. On another occasion, when Hugo was arrested and taken to Cusco, the peasants blockaded the bus he was on, forcing his release (Blanco 1975a: 15).

## The uprising begins

During the early 1960s the *campesinos* were increasingly organised across La Convención and their most dynamic section was to be found in Hugo Blanco's neighbourhood of Chaupimayo. Militant action took the form of strikes, mass meetings and occupations. There was no master plan for insurrection put together by either the *campesinos* or Hugo Blanco or other youthful leftists, instead the movement went through a number of stages, which ended in victory for the peasants. First, the unions would undertake a temporary strike, known as a *paro*. This work stoppage would be used to demand that an eviction was reversed, a contract kept or feudal demands for unpaid work reduced. *Gamonales* would instruct the police to arrest *campesinos* who were active in these campaigns. In response more strikes would be called until they were released. Strikes were easy for the *campesinos* because they were refusing to do work which was unpaid, and unlike industrial workers they also had access to crops they grew themselves. All out strikes (*huelgas*) might also be used to challenge the landowners.

Hugo Blanco believed that mass meetings mobilising thousands of Quechua speakers in Cusco city were vital to raise the self-confidence of the indigenous people. The racist system where the Spanish speaking population dominated the indigenous was described by Hugo as 'the monster' (Blanco

1977: 47). Fearful of the white people, who they called the *misti*, the *campesinos* had been cowed and silent when they visited the city. At mass meetings, the air was thick with the smell of the coca that the Andean indigenous chewed, and the sound of Quechua. Beyond the demands of any particular mass meeting, this gain in cultural confidence contributed to significant social change in the region.

As the occupations grew Hugo Blanco attempted to construct a system of dual power. Trotsky's concept of dual power means creating institutions that rival state structures, contributing to eventual revolution. In Chaupimayo and the rest of La Convención, the Peruvian state was weak, and institutional power was in the hands of the *gamonales*. A landowner had the power of a medieval English lord, able to appoint officials, have roads and other public works built and to administer 'justice'. Increasingly the indigenous took on these roles, raising funds, building schools and staffing them with teachers, while qualified and thus certified by the Peruvian state, appointed by local people. Hugo Blanco felt that Trotsky's notion of dual power could, in a Peruvian context, draw upon the inspiration of the *ayllu*, the indigenous collective that could be traced to pre-*Tawantinsuyu* times. Hugo Blanco's vision, like that of Mariátegui, was of a deepening indigenous socialist system, applying Marxist concepts in a Peruvian context.

In Chaupimayo, Hugo and his comrades called a nine-month strike. They lifted the strike with a declaration of agrarian reform which proclaimed that those who worked the land owned the land. Hugo was aware that land reform in Chaupimayo was insufficient to succeed in gaining land rights across a whole region and knew that the struggle had to be widened. The peasants across La Convención took strike action in protest against a police massacre in the town of Pasco, but the ever-cautious FTC, under pressure from the authorities, helped to end this strike. However the *gamonales* insisted that work lost in the strike be made up. Hugo noted that this was too much for unions who had been 'more or less moderate before', so this increased their militancy and they were persuaded to join a sustained strike *(huelga)* for agrarian reform (Blanco 2018a: 32).

The shift in strike action from specific local grievances to a demand for an end to the neofeudal system led, unsurprisingly, to an angry response from the landowning elite. The *gamonales* armed themselves and threatened the *campesinos*. When assaulted by the landowners and their lackeys, the *campesinos*, as usual, gained little sympathy or protection from the police. As violence against them increased the *campesinos* prepared themselves. The *campesinos* were armed already with carbines that they used to protect themselves against the various wild animals including bears and 'a large fierce breed of guinea pig' (Ward 2010: 657). In Chaupimayo training was undertaken and the example of the *montoneros* was used to enthuse the *campesinos*. The *montoneros* were a militia established by the *gamonales* made up of local people who fought in disputes in the nineteenth century and at the beginning of the twentieth century. Hugo noted too that the Cuban revolution also inspired the indigenous people to arm themselves and organise. Hugo used two pamphlets for training, one from Che and another written by Alberto Bayo, a Cuban revolutionary who had fought in the Spanish Civil War during the 1930s (Blanco 2018a: 35).

During a strike in Huyro, with the odds in their favour, members of Hugo Blanco's militia disarmed both the police and the landowners. The police told them that if they did not return the guns, their commanding officers would call for strong military action, so the weapons were returned to the police but not to the landowners (Blanco 2018a: 34). Alfredo Romainville's cattle were taken, butchered and their meat was sold to buy more weapons for the cause. Some landowners, faced with such rising militancy, agreed to land reform, giving most of the land to the indigenous in return for retaining a little for themselves. Yet as Hugo noted, the atmosphere was becoming tenser by the day (Blanco 2018a: 36). The uprising involved dimensions of property rights, social class and ethnicity. Another element of oppression was gender.

## Women and revolution

Today Peru remains a patriarchal society but at the time of the uprising women did not even have the right to vote. In pre-*Tawantinsuyu* society women did have greater status, often acting as rulers, and the most important deity, the Pachamama, was a goddess. *Tawantinsuyu* society was ruled by the Inka, an exclusively male position, diminishing the equality that had existed. Spanish rule and the introduction of the Catholic religion reduced the status of women more dramatically (Starn 1999: 162).

Hugo felt that women were both the most exploited group in La Convención and also the most militant; the 'first to get arms was a peasant woman who disarmed a policeman in a confrontation with the police and brought his gun back to the village'. (Blanco 1971a: 14). The women with guns were photographed and used for propaganda purposes. Men were armed routinely; as agricultural workers they used guns as a tool for hunting. Armed women in contrast were an unambiguous symbol of insurrection. It was also unheard of at the time for women to act as leaders, but this too changed.

In Huadquina the *campesinos* complained bitterly to Hugo that they lacked a leader for their local union. He told them that they were wrong, 'that they had a very qualified leader among them whom they could elect as their president – the woman who was complaining the most'. (Blanco 1971a: 14) They elected her first as assistant general secretary. Hugo noted that she was one of the most effective leaders of a union; he felt that the oppression of women within *campesino* society weakened the uprising but noted that the women were consistently, as the most oppressed, also the most militant.

When women were trained to use weapons, none of the men dared to object, a special women's commission was formed to support improvements in their status. Campesino union marches in Cusco contained all female sections (Blanco 1971a: 14). While Hugo Blanco as a Trotskyist viewed the working class as the vanguard, which might in some circumstances lead to a focus on white men, questions of gender and ethnicity shaped his approach, deepening his militancy and that of those he worked with. In 1965 women were finally given the vote in Peru.

## The left and the *campesinos*

While unionisation was deepening in the countryside, the city-based left was beginning to take an interest in peasant mobilisations. In the late 1950s, according to Hugo Blanco, the POR (in its Moreno form) in Peru was a tiny organisation. It had fewer than ten members in Lima and a few more in Arequipa, the country's second most populous city (Blanco 1977: 36). Yet the growth of interest in the Cuban revolution meant that, after 1959, youthful activists were increasingly excited by the possibility of guerrilla movements and rural militancy, rather than being drawn to APRA or the far from dynamic Communist Party in Peru. Ironically, this growth was to have dire consequences for Hugo, contributing to the chain of events that led to his lengthy imprisonment during the 1960s.

The Revolutionary Left Front (*Frente de Izquierda Revolucionaria* FIR) was created uniting the Morenoist POR, the Communist Party (Leninist) a group who had left the official Communist Party, and others on the left in 1961 (Alexander 1973: 168). The FIR did not seem to have been built on a particularly strong basis and proved incapable of creating effective, sustained support for Hugo's work. FIR members decided that in order to grow further they would need to fundraise, and rather than the mundane means used by most political organisations such as selling jam or raffle tickets, they decided to take a more direct route: bank robbery. The first bank robbery, in December 1961 from the Banco Popular, saw 105,000 soles (worth at the time approximately $4000) stolen, but nearly half the notes were new and could easily be traced by the police. In April 1962 three million soles (about \$120,000) was stolen from a second Lima bank. Taking the money to Cusco, the FIR members were stopped by the police, Daniel Pereyra opened fire and the others escaped. The bank robbers were soon caught, and the organisation was effectively destroyed in Peru (Gott 1973: 384-386). Hugo did not oppose bank robberies on ethical grounds, but he felt that the tactic was difficult to justify and led to a dangerous reaction from the authorities.

## Lucha armada

From April 1962 to his capture in May 1963, Hugo entered the guerrilla phase of his campaign. The uprising had attracted the attention of the authorities, while the bank robberies in Lima triggered Hugo's pursuit. The Cusco chief of police Humberto Quea openly declared that he would repress the movement first in the capital city, then advance into La Convención and finally occupy Chaupimayo, where Hugo and his friends were training the most robust *campesinos* in military defence. Hugo posted armed guards in Chaupimayo, spent some time away in the mountains, and when he was living in the area changed address regularly to make capture more difficult (Blanco 1977: 64).

Shots were fired by the police during a meeting in Cusco, killing 'Comrade Remigio Huamán'. Assaulted in the countryside, the unions went underground and military preparation accelerated. Hugo recounts how dynamite was bought. A local foreman on a road project was asked if he would sell it to them; he asked whether it was for fishing, and when told that its purpose was military preparation for the *campesinos*, insisted that he supply it for free, throwing in detonators and fuses too (Blanco 2018a: 36-37). *The Internationalist* reported:

> the military junta which seized power in Peru has sent several regiments into the region armed with airplanes and helicopters supplied by the U.S. But thanks to widespread support among the peasant communities of the descendants of the Incas, Hugo Blanco's guerrilla fighters have evaded capture up to now.
>
> Hugo Blanco is immensely popular in Peru today and his fame as a promising young revolutionary leader is spreading throughout Latin America. (Anon 1963a: 3)

During this time Hugo met Blanca:

> Blanca la Barrera was a politically active woman who admired Hugo a lot for his work. Therefore she went to La Convención to find him when he was persecuted and could not leave the valley. They had a son Hugo.

Blanca and Hugo never lived together as he was imprisoned. (Comment from Gunilla Berglund August 2018)

Hugo's son Hugo eventually moved to Spain, as an adult. He became a successful business person until the economic crisis in 2008, after which he moved to the UK, where he lives in 2018 (Interview August 2018 with Oscar Blanco Berglund). Back in the early 1960s his father was facing some drama.

Tiburcio Bolaños, secretary-general of the union in Qayara, told Hugo that while he was away the local *gamonal*, accompanied by a policeman, had ransacked his home and shot an eleven-year-old boy, to try to find out where Bolaños was. Bolaños asked Hugo how he could get justice, to which Hugo replied that justice via the official legal system was impossible. Instead, Hugo and other militants formed a commission to visit the *gamonal*. The commission was essentially an armed militia (Blanco 2018a: 37).

The commission passed a police post in Pujiura. The Civil Guard (CG) officer stationed at the post was invited to let them pass, but he pulled out his gun. A fire fight began, and Hugo shot him. A nurse was found to help him but the officer later died. Hugo knew that authorities would ramp up their attempts to capture him. The officer was the same individual who had shot the eleven-year-old boy. Critical of militarism Hugo noted that his group were 'revolutionaries who fired only to prevent enemy bullets from wounding us, and who treated a wounded enemy as a brother.' (Blanco 1977: 78).

The commission never reached the home of the *gamonal*, but it was later discovered that he had already fled to Cusco (Blanco 1977: 70). The peasantry did all they could to support Hugo Blanco and other members of the Remigio Huamán commission, named after the comrade who had been shot dead in Cusco. Their support, according to Hugo, 'was almost absolute', feeding, clothing and hiding the guerrillas. The peasants, after participating in years of strikes, protests and negotiations with the *gamonales*, were deeply committed to the struggle for land (Blanco 1977: 72). The peasants also engaged in acts of sabotage, such as cutting telegraph wires and destroying bridges to help the commission avoid capture. Hugo continued to act as secretary-general of the peasants' federation and signed the following decree for land reform:

1.  The General Assembly of each union shall nominate an 'agrarian reform commission' form within itself.

2.  The tenants (*arrendires*) and sub-tenants (*allegados*) are automatically converted into owners of the land they work.

3.  Uncultivated land is to be distributed in plots, beginning with the poorest peasants.

4.  Lands in which plantations have been planted for the owner shall remain in his power, provided that his attitude has not been characterized by a human outrage. If it has, these cultivations, and possibly the hacienda-house, shall pass collectively into the power of the union to be used as a school, etc.

5.  The authorities in the service of the bosses may not intervene, for the only people who understand agrarian reality properly are the peasants themselves. (Gott 1973: 388).

This land decree was implemented in the following years, transforming the lives of the *campesinos*, but for Hugo life was becoming difficult. On the run, malaria became as much of a threat as capture. There were two more armed incidents with the police, in one two police officers were killed. The second incident led the remaining members of the commission to scatter in different directions. Hugo was now on his own.

His pursuit continued and despite the help from the *campesinos*, things became more and more challenging. He recounts sleeping in torrential rain, getting up and wringing the water out of his clothes and blanket, sleeping a little longer and repeating the process. On occasions his daily food ration was just nine cabbage leaves, or a little cornmeal stirred into drinking water. He was increasingly in a state of hunger and fever, thinking how foolish it was to wash plates but better, like the peasant children, to lick them clean, or less rationally speculating that clouds were edible (Blanco 1975a: 16).

Eventually the authorities captured and tortured a young peasant who had been helping to shelter him. They surrounded the area where he was hiding and captured him. He was lucky not to be killed on the spot, as was the fate of Che Guevara in Bolivia and many other guerrillas.

The uprising continued after Hugo's arrest, and land occupations spread across Peru. New guerrilla forces active in 1965 were easily defeated but the system of land ownership was transformed (Gott 1973: 458). The peasants had broken the system and successive Peruvian governments, with mixed results, institutionalised land reform. An early academic account of the uprising noted that it had been entirely successful. In La Convención, the *campesinos* defeated the *gamonales*:

From a traditional structure of hacienda social relations, the entire valley, through these events, was transformed into a new system of small landowners (*minifundistas*) who were completely independent of their former masters. In a period of ten years a three-hundred-year-old feudalistic system of social relationships was overthrown and supplanted by organized independent campesinos engaged in the growing of coffee as a cash crop. The hacendados, in the absence of the traditional cheap labor of the tenant farmers, have been forced to find new ways of developing their land or be forced out of business. (Craig 1969: 276)

Hugo role had been to work with the existing movement so as to 'vastly expand, redirect, and intensify it.' (Loveman and Davies 1985: 310). When he was imprisoned, the movement was strong enough to be self-sustaining and thus to achieve its central demands. Hugo Blanco had 'fallen' but the uprising he had contributed to ended in victory, gaining land and dignity for the *campesinos*. He was to spend the rest of the 1960s behind bars. Chapter Four will outline his prison years.

4

# Capture and Cat Lives 1963-1970

'The condor is a wild animal, but the rooster is domesticated. I'd rather be a condor than a rooster'. Hugo Blanco (Hamilton 2017)

From his capture in May 1963 to his release in 1970, Hugo Blanco was imprisoned, for much of the period in the bleak island jail of El Frontón. This chapter covers his capture, trial and imprisonment, along with the huge international campaign to save his life.

## A whisker from death

During his life, Hugo has come close to death on many occasions. He remarked once that the Peruvian cat has seven lives and the Swedish cat has nine, but he has beaten them both. Not counting his fourteen hunger strikes, he listed ten times when he cheated death by a whisker. The first was in La Convención when a landowner had hired a man to kill him, the would-be assassin did not know what Hugo looked like, so took along a *campesino* who did:

> They waited to ambush me on a verge by the road. When I passed by with a group of comrades, the thug asked the *campesino*: 'Is it the one in the straw hat?' It was me but when he saw me the *campesino* felt guilty for taking the bribe and said: 'It's not him.'
> I found out about this months later when the *campesino* himself told me. (Blanco 2018a: 133).

The second brush with death was while Hugo and his comrades were pursued by the authorities. As they discussed who would be the lookout, the police attacked. Hugo noted that he and his friends were only just learning to be guerrillas; later when he was imprisoned in their barracks, the police told him that they were only just learning to be repressors, so had shot blindly and were more concerned with hiding. Amateur repressors had failed to kill trainee guerrillas.

His third listed near death experience was when he was captured in May 1963. It was only by chance that he wasn't immediately assassinated. His story would have ended in similar circumstances to Che Guevara, who was shot after being captured in Bolivia in October 1967 (Gott 1973: 554). The Civil Guard (CG) saw it as a point of honour to execute anyone who had killed one of their number, which, of course, included Hugo. Luckily Hugo was tracked down by their rivals, the Peruvian Investigations Police (PIP), who gave the order that he should be taken alive:

> Chance had it that the one who saw me first was a member of the PIP. He shouted: 'Here he is!' I heard a voice order him: 'Shoot!' This was the chief of the CG. The PIP man shot, but the other way, and in a low voice asked me: 'Do you surrender?' From down on the ground where I had thrown myself I said 'yes'. The policeman was nervous. He told me: 'Show your hands! Keep still!'
>
> They say there are some people who do not know fear; I am not one of them. I have been afraid many times, sometimes over ridiculous things. But, fortunately, at crucial movements, I am calm. (Blanco 2018a: 134)

Hugo surrendered, handing over his dagger and pistol. The CG officer approached him with hate in his eyes, and struck him with a rifle butt, splitting his head open. Shouting at him, the officer accused Hugo of killing three of his colleagues. Later, PIP men revealed to Hugo that the Civil Guard officer had been told by other members of his force that he should have killed both Hugo and the PIP officer, lying that they had all died as result of an exchange of fire!

Hugo was barefoot and the PIP officer asked him where his shoes were. His shoes were hidden along with documents that he didn't want the authorities to see, so he insisted that he had none. He asked them whether they would hang him, a form of torture, in Quillabamba, Cusco or Lima. They told him that this was unnecessary, 'We hung up people to find where you were; we don't need to ask you that'. He was driven to the nearest town, shaved and given shoes. People seeing him applauded and he shouted, 'Land or Death!' He was flown by helicopter to Cusco, in great haste, to prevent local people from setting him free. He remarked on how beautiful the thickly wooded valley of Vilcanota appeared from the helicopter (Blanco 2018a: 134–135).

### Fraternising with the enemy

The helicopter took him to a barracks outside of Cusco, where he was interrogated day and night for a month. Worried that he was fraternising with his guards, and that they might become sympathetic to him and even aid an escape bid, the prison authorities replaced them with a more repressive group, the assault officers. Suspicion grew that the assault officers were unduly friendly with him, so they were again replaced with members of the supposedly more hard-line mounted police, who were forbidden to talk to Hugo. Many police and soldiers were drawn from the Quechua-speaking population, so potentially sympathetic and Hugo is a genial individual who is difficult not to like. After a month in the barracks, he was delivered to Prision Siglo XX in the southern city of Arequipa (Blanco 1975a: 17).

He was placed in solitary confinement; communication with comrades from La Convención, who were also imprisoned in Prision Siglo XX, was forbidden. Many *campesino* organisers, including other Trotskyists, were also held. Hugo and these other politicals went on hunger strike. This succeeded, and they were allowed to speak to each other without punishment. Prison visits were restricted for a time to priests, nuns and members of US peace corps. Eventually, close relatives were allowed, but Hugo was told that his brother was not close enough to be allowed to see him. Visitors were accompanied by three security staff (Blanco 1975a: 17).

Correspondence from outside the prison could only be brought in by visitors, and any letters had to be presented at least a day before the visit, so it could be copied three times. Even drawings from Hugo's five-year-old daughter Carmen were copied. Some of the guards seem to have taken delight in making life uncomfortable for the prisoners, Hugo noted how some nights he would be woken every couple of hours with a flash light. Bizarrely, the toys that the prisoners made to be sold to the outside world could not be painted in certain ways. Hugo and his comrades liked to watch the other prisoners playing football in the yard, but the window they looked through was blocked by a steel plate (Blanco 1975a: 17). It is worth remembering that these events occurred in the summer of 1964, and that Hugo was to endure difficult prison conditions throughout the rest of the 1960s and into the 1970s.

The international campaign to free him began within days of his capture. On 15 May 1963, the Fourth International launched protests insisting that 'Hugo Blanco is guilty of no crime but that of a heroic effort to liberate the peasants in the Peruvian Andes from their age-old ·servitude and feudal-capitalist exploitation' (Anon 1963b: 5). Supporters were urged to send letters and telegrams to the Peruvian government. It was reported that two demonstrations for Hugo's freedom had taken place at the Peruvian Embassy in London. One organised by the newly founded 'Release Hugo Blanco Committee' and the other by the Socialist Labour League (Anon 1963b: 5).

*The Internationalist* reported in July 1963 that members of the Ceylon (Sri Lankan) parliament had sent telegrams demanding Hugo Blanco's release and that further demonstrations had taken place in Japan and Canada. *The Militant,* the paper of the US Socialist Workers Party, informed readers that a demonstration called by the Young Socialist Alliance for 27 July was to be held at the Peruvian Consulate in New York. The protest was supported by the Puerto Rican Movimiento Pro-Independencia. Fearing that Hugo had been injured, demonstrators were to demand that he was 'transferred to a hospital and be allowed to see family; friends and defense counsel' (Anon 1963c: 1). A worldwide movement was growing but it would be many years before it would achieve its goal of freedom for Hugo.

The arrest of Hugo Blanco did nothing to reduce the militancy of the peasant movement. In December 1963 the British journalist Norman Gall wrote that '5,000 of his followers marched on Cuzco, enforcing a general strike and destroying a bridge, telegraph lines, and train rails' (Gall 1967: 67). As well as protesting his continuing imprisonment, land occupations had spread across ever larger areas of Peru. In Hugo's home district of Huanoquite, where Bartolome Paz had branded Francisco Zamata with a red-hot iron, *campesinos* armed with Mausers and 22 calibre pistols 'engaged in a bloody battle' at Paz's *hacienda* in November 1963 (Seligmann 1995: 57). *World Outlook,* a Fourth International publication, reported in December 1963 that:

> The peasants of Rio Huallaga took over a considerable area of land on September 2. During the same month, 2,000 communalists of Yanacocha occupied 900 hectares (one hectare = 2.47 acres) in Huaratambo. At Huaylacucho four haciendas (large-estates) were taken over. At Huancay 3,000 communalists invaded the Moro hacienda, a holding of the imperialist company Cerro de Pasco. They occupied 500 hectares of the property. At Yacta, communalists, shouting, 'Land or death!'
> occupied the Corpacancha hacienda. Police killed Adrian M. Hidalgo. In the north of Peru, peasants seized the Huabal estate and some others in the district of Canchaqui. Other occupations took place at Jauga, Puno. (Anon 1963d: 14–15)

In February 1964 Hugo's sister Luchy was arrested for her part in helping the peasants of Sicuani to reclaim their ancestral land and sent to prison in the Amazon. Eight thousand *campesinos* took part, unarmed. Seventeen of them were killed when the landowner and his followers opened fire (Anon 1964: 1).

## Court appearances

The authorities, fearful of public support for Hugo, waited three years before putting him on trial in 1966. His lawyers, Victor Angeles and Alfredo Battilana, were both jailed for a time (Blanco 1977: 77). Pressure was placed on his co-defendants to denounce him in return for freedom or shorter sentences. Proceedings took place in Tacna, a town near the Chilean border, far from Cusco, because it was felt that holding it in a location where he was better known would lead to supporters mobbing proceedings. The trial, taking the form of a military tribunal, was held in the Civil Guards headquarters. During the times when Hugo was able to communicate with his co-defendants he told them that they should insist that they were innocent and should state, 'We are semiliterate *campesinos* who were deceived by the Communist Hugo Blanco'.

On the first day of the hearing it was clear that they had not done so; Hugo and the other accused were overjoyed to see each other after so long apart, hugging with great affection (Blanco 2018a: 44). Hugo approached the hearing confidently, arguing that the Civil Guards should be on trial, not him or his comrades, because they were guilty of murder, killing and persecuting *campesinos* on behalf of the *gamonales*. At the end of the first session he shouted, *Tierra o Muerte!* to which the other accused responded with a loud cry of *Venceremos!* ('We shall overcome').

Despite the three-year gap since his arrest and the fact that the trial was held in a small town remote from Cusco, whose citizens were largely middle-class merchants unlikely to be sympathetic to guerrillas and revolutionaries, public interest grew with each day of the hearing. So too did media attention both in Peru and internationally.

The *campesino* uprising and the obvious abuse that had led to it made condemning Hugo and his comrades difficult. During the trial, the prosecution tried to build a case that, while it was wrong to take up arms, support for land reform was justified. Hugo noted that his prosecutors praised him 'to the skies' and lauded his work to improve the health, education and general conditions of the peasants who had been so abused. The violence used to defend the *campesinos* was condemned by the prosecutors (Blanco 2018a: 45).

The trial continued with Hugo and his lawyers mounting a strong legal and political defence. Alfredo Battilana, released by this time, drew attention to the many flaws in the proceedings. For example, witnesses such as the surviving police and the nurse who had treated the officer shot by Hugo had not been allowed to testify during the trial.

Hugo, when called to the stand, admitted that he had lied on one matter.

Two other police had been killed in shoot outs; he insisted after his capture that he had shot both of them, not wanting to incriminate other members of the commission. The ballistics report at the trial showed that neither officer had been shot with Hugo's weapon but, as he claimed responsibility for the deaths at the time, this inconsistency in the evidence had been ignored (Blanco 2018a: 45).

His lawyer asked Hugo what he had told Tiburcio Bolaños to do when his home was ransacked, whether he had referred him to some authority that could help him. This question enabled Hugo to outline in some detail the failure of the official legal system to protect the *campesinos* from the abusive power of the *gamonales*. With no legal system operating in their defence, the *campesinos'* only alternative was to take direct action. Hugo noted that the police were Indians too. Commanded by cowardly officers who hid behind their desks and the Civil Guards, they had been instructed to murder other Indians as part of a system that supported the powerful (Blanco 2018a: 45). Hugo was required by the court to make concrete points of fact and to avoid polemical statements. Yet by answering questions calmly he raised a powerful political case, outlining the abusive nature of the exercise of law in La Convención.

Hugo's lawyer asked that the court try him for subversion, as he had issued laws without having the state power to do so. Asked if this was true, Hugo answered that indeed it was, describing the 'Agrarian Reform Law' that he had issued. General Fernando Hernani had, Hugo's lawyer revealed, called for the death penalty. Hugo, who was allowed to respond after his questioning, insisted that if the penalty for the land reform that had occurred in La Convención was death, he would willingly agree to be executed. He added that since the Civil and Republican Guard members were as 'sons of the people', their hands should not be stained with his blood. Instead the General himself should carry out his execution. Hugo helpfully pointed out General Hernani, who was in the courtroom (Blanco 1977: 80).

The court proceedings seem to have gradually won over the people of Tacna who had gone to witness the murder trial of a notorious Communist agitator but had come to sympathise with the plight of the peasants. By this point they had begun to applaud Hugo's lawyer. When Hugo finished speaking and ended with his cry of *Tierra o Muerte!* many of the townspeople responded with a shout of '*Venceremos!*' (Blanco 2018a: 46). The newspaper *Tacera* published a special issue about the trial, helping to convince local people of Hugo's case (Blanco 1977: 81).

Hoping that the local people would get tired of waiting, Hugo and his comrades were not taken from the court to their cells until the middle of the night, but many locals remained until they could applaud their exit (Blanco 1977: 81). The next day, when visitors were allowed, long queues formed of sympathisers, who gave many gifts including fruit that was shared between the prisoners. One man tried to give a lawyer a coat as a gift to Hugo (Blanco 2018a: 46).

Hugo was careful to explain to the officers guarding him that he made a distinction between them and their commanders, thus by the end of his trial they were very much on his side:

> My jailers, members of the Republican Guard, already knew who I was and their support for me was total. When I stood up to rebuke the court, if some official was nearby they said: 'Sit down!' – pretending to make an effort to get me to sit down, so that I seemed like a wild man. When the officials went away they would say: 'Shout more at that miserable lot, Huguito!' They brought pictures in which we appeared together and asked me to sign them. (Blanco 2018a: 46-47)

The court rejected the death penalty but sentenced Hugo to twenty-five year in prison. His lawyers appealed, and the public prosecutor responded by calling for his execution to be reinstated. Seven co-defendants who were also on trial for militancy wrote a letter insisting that if Hugo was executed, they must be executed with him:

> If he is to be shot, they asked, let them be permitted to stand at his side and be shot at the same time. The news of this action was reported in *Le Monde* of November 26. The Paris daily also reported that political prisoners of all kinds in Peru have gone on a hunger strike to express solidarity with Hugo Blanco. Students in a number of universities have called strikes as a way of showing support for him. According to another source in Paris, the Pentagon is placing pressure on Belaúnde to go ahead and execute the popular peasant leader. (Anon 1966: 1)

The new call for a death sentence was defeated, in 1967, by the work of Hugo's lawyer and the solidarity of a growing international campaign to save him from execution. Ultimately Hugo was sentenced to twenty-five-years imprisonment, at the time the maximum, while his co-defendants were set free because they had already spent time behind bars or given just a few years. The trial had been another stage in the uprising; from strikes, to occupation, to self-defence to guerrilla action, the legal battle had been another blow struck against the now collapsing neo-feudal system in La Convención.

The campaign to save Hugo's life had been pioneered by the Fourth International, which had reunited in 1963, supported by a wider variety of groups and famous individuals. They argued that it was not necessary to agree with Hugo to defend him, it was enough to oppose his execution. Although Amnesty International refused to give support to those involved in violence, they recognised Hugo's plea of self-defence and were vigorous in their support. The Swedish section of Amnesty made Hugo their prisoner of the year (Blanco 2018a: 47). A vast number of celebrities from across the globe joined the campaign against Hugo's execution.

Several meetings were held in London, organized by the Committee for Solidarity with the Victims of Repression in Peru. The philosopher and peace activist Bertrand Russell agreed to be honorary President:

> The committee has the support of many prominent individuals, including Mrs. Harold Laski, Isaac Deutscher, Bill Molloy M.P., Syd Bidwell M.P., Hamza Halevi and Ernie Roberts of the Amalgamated Engineering Union (in his personal capacity).
>
> The campaign was launched at well-attended meeting in London's Caxton Hall, with Roger Protz, editor of *Labour Worker*, in the chair. The principal speaker was Bill Molloy, Labour M.P. for Ealing North, who has been very active in the cause of Hugo Blanco and who has had several interviews with the Peruvian ambassador on his behalf. (Anon 1967a: 649)

A pamphlet entitled 'Land or Death- the case of Hugo Blanco' was sold along with red and gold badges with the words 'FREE LIBRE HUGO BLANCO', costing nine pence each.

The Peruvian campaign was also strong with strikes and rallies being held on his behalf. Hugo suspected that President Belaúnde, who had been elected in 1963, replacing the previous military juntas, would use a plea for clemency from Hugo and his family as a propaganda opportunity (Blanco 2018a: 48). So, Hugo wrote a letter, read out at a rally in Lima, rejecting a pardon from the President. Ultimately all of this campaigning saved Hugo's life, but he was to remain in prison until 1970. *World Outlook* reported in October 1967 that while Hugo's death sentence had been lifted, the campaign for his freedom would continue:

> The decision of the court, rejecting the demand of the prosecution to kill Hugo Blanco, represents a victory for the international campaign waged in his behalf. However, it is only a partial victory. Hugo Blanco still faces

a quarter of a century in prison because of his revolutionary-socialist views. The campaign to win his freedom will certainly be continued. The partial victory gained should serve to intensify the demands to President Belaúnde to grant amnesty to Hugo Blanco and his comrades who are in prison with him. (Anon 1967b: 861)

The strength of his defence, together with an international solidarity campaign, saved Hugo from execution; two more of his cats' lives had been spent.

## El Frontón

El Frontón is an island prison on Peru's Pacific coast, near Lima, described in 1969 as waterless, bitterly 'cold in winter and unbearably hot in summer' (Cooper 1969: 183). It was almost impossible to escape from, although Belaúnde, who had been held briefly in El Frontón as political prisoner in 1959, had attempted to swim to the mainland without success. Hugo noted that when he was taken there it contained two thousand prisoners, described by the authorities as 'the most dangerous of all criminals'. Initially he was once again placed in solitary confinement and once again went on a hunger strike to win the right to leave his cell during the day. He described it as a 'notorious hell' (Blanco 1975a: 17).

Murders occurred on a regular basis, usually over trivial issues committed by a population of inmates who had been seriously damaged by Peruvian society. Health care was extremely poor; once suffering severe illness, Hugo checked in to the infirmary to find that the medicines had been stolen and resold by prison officials. Drinking water was taken from a well with buckets contaminated with human excrement. Those with mental illness were treated particularly badly, as were gay prisoners who were 'prostituted and humiliated' (Blanco 1975a: 17). When in 2010 Hugo Blanco stayed with me in Britain, many years and thousands of miles away from this desperate island prison, he told me that he was happy to sleep on my floor because he had slept on concrete blocks, so it would be no hardship to him! I was happy, in my small space, of course, to give my guest the bed and to sleep on the floor myself. It was one small reminder of another minor misery of El Frontón.

Prisoners were often tortured in a chamber known as the House of Dracula, or taken to the pier, hung by their feet and dipped head first in the sea, threatening drowning. Escape attempts provoked the prison authorities into beating the prisoners. The prisoners were goaded with various forms of cruelty in the hope that they would mutiny, which would then be used to justify machine-gunning those who rebelled (Blanco 1975a: 17).

A Lima supporter of Hugo Blanco wrote in 1968 that his situation was 'very, very dangerous'. A prisoner had been killed with impunity, he was:

> an insane person who wandered into a forbidden zone to answer the call of nature. He was riddled with bullets in front of everybody. He didn't do anything or say anything. You can imagine the atmosphere of terror reigning in El Frontón [...] If those in command in El Frontón want to liquidate Hugo Blanco, they can do so without any scruple and no one could interfere. (Anon 1968: 376)

It was feared later in 1968 that Hugo had been murdered by prison guards in such an incident. Hugo Bravo and another prisoner were beaten to death after an escape attempt, and some individuals had confused the identities of the two Hugos. Hugo Blanco wrote a letter exposing the murders, drawing upon eyewitnesses and naming the guilty:

> When the prisoners fell during beatings, the guards forced them with kicks to get up and heel. Hugo Bravo fell limp. They threw water on him, they stamped on him, but he didn't get up again. 'Ojon' shouted, 'Let me go, I'm strangling,' and tried to get up. The guards forced him back down on his knee with kicks. 'Call the nurse, I'm dying,' he said, his voice breaking, and he fell, blood pouring from his mouth.
> (Blanco 1968: 838)

The international outcry over Hugo Blanco's letter may have saved his life, along with others, but he and Eduardo Creus, who he had first met in Argentina at the Swift meat packing plant in the 1950s, were beaten in front of other prisoners as yet another provocation to mutiny.

Hugo noted that his bleakest day was seeing a prisoner being led away to be executed. Observing this, and meditating on a system that brutalises people, turns some of them into criminals, who it tortures and then sometimes kills, upset him deeply. His hatred of the system was so intense he couldn't sleep (Blanco 1975a: 17).

Despite the horrors, Hugo Blanco was allowed some visitors. One of the first foreign visitors was Kitty Cone, a US campaigner for disability rights who arrived in 1967. She visited Hugo's mother, met the Cusco chief of police, like many members of police an admirer, and travelled to the island prison:

When my cousin and I got to Cuzco, we found Hugo's mother and gave her a bouquet of roses. She was very, very thrilled that people from another country were supporting her son. It was kind of interesting, because the person who had taken us under his wing in Cuzco was the police chief, and he had great admiration for Hugo Blanco. That to me was astonishing. He took us to find Hugo's mother. Anyway, she gave us the name of his cousin in Lima. When we got to Lima we looked him up, and at first he was very dubious about having anything to do with two Americans, but when he realized that Hugo's mother had sent us and that we were innocent radicals, he invited us into his home and gave us gifts, pieces of art that Hugo had made. He arranged for me to go and visit Hugo. (Cone 2000: 59-60).

She gave Hugo an English language copy of Isaac Deutscher's three volume biography of Trotsky along with other books. Hugo told her that she and her cousin were the first Americans to visit El Frontón, presenting them with 'carved wooden, Andean dressed cartoon caricatures of birds that he had made, and he gave each of us a wooden turtle that was a jewelry box.' (Cone 2000: 60). She described the sea crossing from Lima as 'perilous'. On her return to the USA she joined the Socialist Workers Party, which at the time was a section of the Fourth International, and strongly supportive of Hugo Blanco.

Peter Camejo (1939-2008), a Venezuelan-American member of the US Socialist Workers Party, visited Hugo in January 1970. Camejo, who ran for the SWP as their US Presidential candidate and later was a prominent member of the Green Party, had worked hard on Hugo's ongoing solidarity campaign. Camejo also edited the English language edition of 'Land or Death' that Hugo had written in prison:

It was such a joyous moment for me to meet him in person. We sat together and talked about all kinds of things, especially the international campaign on his behalf. [...] Unfortunately visitors were only allowed one hour. The guards strode through the jail, announcing that the visitors' boat was about to leave. I was not about to limit my meeting with Blanco to a single hour, so I hid in the prison until they left. Since the guards had not even counted the visitors upon arrival, they had no idea one remained behind. Blanco told me 'Don't worry, they won't arrest you. There is a prison guard change at 4 p.m. and you can get on that boat and leave.' We talked for several more hours, completely unnoticed by the guards.

That was the beginning of a close friendship and political collaboration (Camejo 2010: 159-160).

On 22 December 1970 Hugo was given an amnesty by the Peruvian government and released. The sudden arrival of freedom was a shock after years of living in police cells, barracks and prison. While he had been able to cope with the miseries and cruelties of El Frontón, he found his release day challenging. He was all too aware of those left in the prison. He noted that international campaign for his release had had several positive results, radicalising many young people; it also forced Peru's government to improve its treatment of prisoners. Events outside of prison in Peru had been moving during Hugo's years of incarceration, and an examination of these is necessary to explain why he was freed at the end of 1970.

## Peru 1963-1970

During the 1960s a vigorous debate ensued on the left about the justifications for guerrilla warfare (Debray 1975, Hansen 1979). Advocates, such as the French author Régis Debray, supported a *foci* strategy. This meant creating a small force of fighters who would inspire others to join their cause. Such a form of propaganda by deed would lead to a wider uprising and eventually the guerrilla forces would grow so large that they would overthrow the dictatorial government that existed in the particular country that the strategy was applied to. This *foci* strategy seemed to have succeeded for Che and Castro in Cuba and the assumption of many leftists in the 1960s was that it could succeed in other parts of Latin America. While some members of the Trotskyist movement had joined or attempted to join the struggle, former Aprist and dissident communists also formed guerrilla movements. In the mid-1960s the hope of some on the left was that, with the example of Hugo Blanco in mind and peasant land occupations continuing, a *foci* strategy could be used to unleash national revolution in Peru.

Luis De La Puente Uceda, from the MIR (*Movimiento de Izquierda Revolucionaria*), made up of former Aprists, had visited Hugo in La Convención in 1962 and asked for cooperation in launching a guerrilla struggle, inspired by the Cuban approach. Hugo had responded that guerrilla activity would only occur if and when the *campesinos* called for it. In 1965 De La Puente launched a guerrilla campaign in La Convención. Luis was captured and killed on the spot and the rest of the MIR were soon defeated. Another guerrilla group, Héctor Béjar's *Ejército de Liberación Nacional* (ELN), met a similar fate (Gott 1973: 446).

The issue of land reform and the obvious racist abuse of the indigenous campesinos was having an impact on Peruvian politics. On 3 October 1968 leftist army officers, led by General Juan Velasco, carried out a successful coup against Belaúnde, whose land reforms had stalled (Werlich 1979: 297). Velasco promised a revolutionary government who would make sweeping changes, Hugo was cautious. He felt that there were gains from the new regime's assault on the *gamonal* system but believed that the land reform promised was bureaucratic and did little to respect the cooperative commons of the *ayllu*, which he saw as the basis for an alternative social system. In the years after the coup Velasco offered to release a number of left-wing political prisoners in return for support.

> Velasco sent me a message. He said if I would agree to work for the agrarian reform, the next day I would be free. But I said 'No thank you, I've gotten used to living in prison.' [Laughs] I could not place myself at the service of a government, because this would be to say that everything this government was doing was good. It is different from being a councilman or a mayor or a congressman or senator, where you can say what you think. If you are working directly for a government, you can't do this. (Weinberg 2009)

Hugo refused this offer, but others such as Héctor Béjar were released and took part in state efforts towards land reform. Finding it difficult to justify releasing Béjar without giving Hugo freedom, Velasco released him too (Blanco 2018a: 49). The early 1970s were yet more years of drama, with Hugo being exiled from Peru and eventually going to live in Chile. He used up another of his cat lives during the 1973 Chilean coup.

# Freedom and Exile 1970-1973

'It's like a handshake coming through a letter. The conscious solidarity of the workers is a great and beautiful thing!' Hugo Blanco (Anon 1971a: 4).

If the 1960s were his prison years, the 1970s were largely those of exile. Freed, he was deported from Peru within months, spending time in Mexico, Argentina, Chile, and after the coup, Sweden.

## A trip to the pharmacy

On 11 January 1971 the Fourth International's English language magazine *Intercontinental Press* proclaimed, 'Campaign for Hugo Blanco ends in great victory'. Visited by his partner Blanca and their seven-year-old son, also named Hugo, on the morning of 22 December 1970, he told them that news of his amnesty was probably a cruel lie. However, the release was confirmed almost immediately and Hugo, along with other freed prisoners, boarded a launch which took them to the mainland. Reaching Lima, Hugo's first act was to visit the central prison office to demand the release of his Argentine comrade Eduardo Creus who remained in El Frontón (Anon 1971a: 3). Hugo's disorientation continued for several days; it was a shock to be free after seven years in captivity. Asked about his plans by journalists, he told them:

> I am not going to return immediately to Cuzco. I have to get over this feeling of disorientation which is almost a physical pain. Although it may not seem to you that I'm telling the truth, I am learning all over again how to see, to hear, to cross the streets (Anon 1971a: 4).

Hugo felt that international solidarity was vital to achieving his release. He thanked those who had campaigned for his freedom:

This solidarity shown by the popular organizations in Lima as well as London or Paris helped me overcome the feeling of loneliness and the difficult hours. It's extraordinary to get messages of support and even checks from people you do not know, written in foreign languages, making you realize that you are not alone! (Anon 1971a: 4).

He pledged his solidarity to other political prisoners, including Basque prisoners held by Franco's dictatorial Spanish regime, and those held in various Latin American prisons by other military governments.

El Comité de Defensa de los Derechos Humanos (CODDEH) held a fiesta on 30 December in Lima. It drew ten thousand people and Hugo Blanco spoke in support of the *campesinos,* calling for further land reform. He made another plea to free Eduardo Creus (Anon 1971a: 4). Creus was a particular concern; they had become friends in Argentina and shared a cell in El Frontón. Creus, the authorities argued, was not a political prisoner but a criminal because of his part in the Lima bank robberies. Creus was freed on 20 January 1971 and immediately deported to Argentina (Camejo 2010: 160). It took a little longer for Hugo Blanco, but he too was to be deported. While the military government had made reforms and proclaimed their left-wing nature, they were nervous about challenges to their authority.

Shortly after gaining his freedom Hugo visited the Peasants' union of Hauando, near Lima, and the miners' union of Casaplaca. After so long in prison he was keen to rejoin the *campesinos* in Cusco province, but the Minister of the Interior banned him from doing so. Asked by a journalist why Hugo Blanco could not travel to Cusco, General Armando Artola of the Ministry of the Interior stated that Blanco could travel 'anywhere', but 'not if he is going to interfere with the agrarian reform'. (Anon 1971b: 78). Students, workers and *campesino* organisations invited him to speak at their mass meetings but he was prevented from doing so. He was able to meet striking miners, in dispute with the Cerro de Pasco Corporation, when they marched through Lima, but the police responded by locking him up for 24 hours (the maximum allowed without being charged) (Blanco 1975a: 17).

Despite proclaiming its revolutionary nature, the Velasco government was in conflict with many groups of workers and *campesinos.* Hugo's continuing opposition to the government, and perhaps most specifically his support for a teachers' strike, eventually led to his deportation from Peru. On 13 September, while visiting his local pharmacy for some medicine, he was approached by two members of the police, who asked him to accompany them to their headquarters. He asked if he could take a blanket with him, aware that the cells could be cold. He was interviewed and treated well, no beatings or threats, but questioned as to why he continued to oppose the government. 'Thus the conversation concerned the agrarian reform and its lack of thoroughness, the class nature of the Velasco regime, and so on' (Blanco 1971b: 809). To his surprise, he was taken from the police headquarters to Lima's Jorge Chávez International Airport and flown out of the country. After stopping in Panama, where he was held in the barracks of the National Guard, a change of flight took him to Mexico City, where he was left with the equivalent of £10 and his blanket. A Mexican government representative drove him to a good hotel, supplied him with more cash and promised him a work permit.

Interviewed by a Mexican newspaper he praised his treatment by the Mexican government:

> This, I would like to note, is in the traditions of Mexico. This country also granted asylum to Trotsky, my teacher, when no other country he went to in the world would accept him. Trotsky always respected the conditions of his asylum, and, although an internationalist, never interfered in the slightest in Mexican politics. (Blanco 1971c: 833)

Hugo's family members, including his children Carmen, aged twelve, and Hugo, aged eight, remained in Peru.

## Argentina

In June 1972 Hugo decided to travel to Argentina. His flight from Mexico refuelled at Lima's Jorge Chavez airport, but he wasn't allowed to leave the international departure lounge. He told journalists, during the stop off on 12 June,

> I am going to Buenos Aires because I will feel closer to Peru there. I have no specific plans, but it is possible that I will give some lectures, as I did in Mexico. I have a visa for Argentina, and I don't know how long I will stay there.

A crowd of his supporters met him during his short stop in Peru:

> We had very short notice that Hugo Blanco would pass through Lima, but this did not prevent his comrades and close associates from gathering to greet him. Stationed on the observation deck of the airport, we anxiously awaited the arrival of the plane from Mexico City.
> The plane arrived at 6:20 a.m. We saw Hugo disembark in the midst of

other passengers, responding to our shouted greetings with the clenched fist salute. Once in the airport waiting room, he was interviewed by several reporters who had come to meet him, and we were able, from the second floor, to speak with him in Spanish and Quechua.

When the stopover was at an end, we watched him leave as he had come: walking with raised fist and looking up defiantly. Filled with emotion and determined anger, we chanted our promise over and over: 'Hugo Blanco Will Return!' (Anon 1972a: 804)

A month after arriving in Argentina, Hugo was informed that he would be deported. Imprisoned on 12 July, the Argentine Socialist Party campaigned for his freedom, plastering Buenos Aires with posters and holding regular press conferences. A campaign was also ongoing in Peru to demand an end to his exile (Thorstad 1972: 883).

Argentina was in the grip of a military regime, which had taken power in 1966 through a coup. The junta had introduced a law allowing them to deport any foreigner who threatened 'national security' within five days. While Hugo had only commented on the situation in Peru, Argentina was in the midst of social conflict, guerrilla fighters were active in the country and the summer of 1972 saw a prison break out, plane hijackings and killings by the state. Hugo was an icon of Marxist militancy and one of the best-known revolutionaries in Latin America, so was far from popular with right-wing military governments like that of Argentina. *Avanzada Socialista*, the newspaper of the Argentine Socialist Party noted:

Hugo Blanco is in prison because his experiences indicate the genuine path of struggle and because, by pointing up the errors of *foquismo* and guerrilla struggle in isolation from the mass movement through his own experience as an armed fighter, he is helping to strengthen the workers and socialist pole and mass mobilizations as the road to victory for the workers and the exploited. (Anon 1972b: 923)

He had spent over three months in prison, noting that conditions in Villa Devoto jail in Buenos Aires 'were awful', 'Physically, they were better than in Peru, but morally speaking they were much worse. The hostility of the guards was terrible' (Nyblom 1973: 1089). The intention, Hugo suggested, was to promote instability, insecurity and powerlessness amongst the political prisoners. Degradation and humiliation were the norm. Gifts from relatives and friends such as radios might be smashed in front of prisoners. Using the pretext of searching for weapons, the prisoners were regularly taken out of their cells, while their property was stolen, broken or scattered over the floor. As lights were left on continuously the only clue to whether it was night or day was the arrival of meals. These were 'lousy'. Rules, for example, as to what books were allowed, were impossible to discern; one day a text by Lenin might be allowed, another day even the Bible would be taken away. Hugo endured long days of boredom with nothing to do or read; the only noises heard were the screams of the tortured and the clanging of the iron gates (Blanco 1975a: 18).

Despite the campaign for his freedom and against deportation gaining the support of the Argentine Trade Union Council and numerous prominent politicians, Hugo was flown to Chile on 26 October 1972. A crowd of a hundred and fifty supporters cheered him at the airport with shouts of 'Viva Hugo Blanco!' (Anon 1972c: 1249).

## The Chilean coup

The General Secretary of the Chilean Socialist Party had helped Hugo to gain a visa, so he could go to Chile when he was deported from Argentina. Right-wing military regimes dominated Latin America by the 1970s, usually with enthusiastic support from the US government, who saw fighting the Cold War and opposing even reformist flavours of socialism as more important than defending human rights and democracy. Chile too was to soon fall to the generals and the CIA. However in 1972 it was governed by socialists and Hugo was to avoid persecution for a time,

> It was very pleasant for me to be in Chile when Allende was president. For the only time in my life I was in a country with a high popular consciousness. Everywhere the workers were organized in unions and these in their corresponding federations: textile, metallurgical, etc. In Chile, in addition to that organization, there was the organization by geographical unit for the development of large mobilizations. The factories in each industrial area, formed an industrial cord: 'Cord Cerrillos', 'Cordón Vicuña Mackenna', etc. I collaborated writing the press organ of the Vicuña Mackenna cord, which I named *El Cordonazo* thinking of El Cordobazo which was a great insurrectionary movement of that time in Córdoba, Argentina. (Interview August 2018)

An interview with a Swedish journalist in 1973, shortly before the coup in Chile, revealed that Hugo was living simply in the capital city of Santiago in an apartment with one room plus a kitchen, which he shared with his ten-year-old son. He spent his days writing articles, but his future was far from secure; his residence permit was due to run out in January 1974 (Nyblom 1973: 1089). Hugo's eldest child Carmen also joined him around this time. While he was able to seek residence in Sweden, he was reluctant to move so far from home, showing considerable homesickness for Cusco and La Convención.

He had been refused entry to every Latin American country other than Chile. Even the Cuban government refused him asylum because they were supportive of the Velasco Peruvian regime. He asked the Peruvian Embassy if he could visit his mother who was near death. This had been refused, even though the authorities had confirmed that she was extremely ill. He observed sadly, 'That was a heavy blow for me', adding 'My mother was the one person I loved most.' (Nyblom 1973: 1089).

The situation in Chile deteriorated during 1973. After several attempts, the veteran socialist politician Salvador Allende became President in 1970. This angered both the USA and Chile's elites. A reformist Christian Democrat President, Eduardo Frei, had already moved the country to the left during the 1960s and Allende's success was seen as a product of long term attempts to construct a democratic socialist alternative. Allende was unique; a Marxist who came to power, not through armed revolution, but via the electoral system. He was elected as part of the Popular Front of parties that included the Socialist, Communist, Social Democratic and Radical Parties. Allende gained the highest number of votes in the 1970 presidential election with 36 per cent, but no President can govern unless they gain 50 per cent of the vote or have the support of the Chilean congress. The Christian Democrats in Congress joined members of the Popular Front and voted for Allende to be confirmed as President (Roxborough et al 1977).

Hugo Blanco was critical of Allende's strategy almost as soon as he was aware of it. Interviewed by Mexican students in December 1972, Hugo observed that Allende's government provided a potential step towards socialism, yet to gain Congressional support, too many compromises with the right had been made. More seriously, he argued, Allende's failure to mobilise mass support would lead eventually to catastrophe:

the army is lying in wait for the right moment to move, to overthrow Allende. It is calculating the relationship of forces, estimating whether or not the popular masses have been sufficiently weakened to permit a coup. Thus, the only way to block these intentions effectively is to mobilize the masses. Clearly Allende is not doing this. He is afraid to do it. For if the masses did mobilize actively against these right-wing manoeuvres, the mobilization would burst beyond the limits Allende, or the leaders of his Unidad Popular, want to impose. Therefore, I think it is the duty of the revolutionary left in Chile to organize the popular masses themselves to resist these rightist schemes, even though Allende opposes such a mobilization [...] Allende is taking this same suicidal attitude, suicidal for him, perhaps, and for his regime (Blanco 1972: 37).

The situation in 1973 was becoming more dangerous. A right-wing group *Patria y Libertad* (Country and Freedom) were actively arming themselves and working to overthrow Allende. Pressure from the USA was leading to food shortages and rampant inflation. On 15 May, the government proclaimed a state of emergency in Santiago, banning demonstrations. The murder of a communist worker, José Ricardo Ahumada, led to tensions, and on 4 May fights broke out between leftist groups and right-wing forces, resulting in the death of one member of *Patria y Libertad* and the wounding of four others.

Strikes were increasing as workers tried to maintain their standards of living while inflation rose. The government was under further strain because while Allende remained President the executive was dominated by the opposition. The government condemned strikes as helping the right; a copper miners' stoppage was challenged by an extension of the emergency zone, two tanks and five hundred soldiers were sent in 'but the miners offered resistance and blocked access roads'. The right claimed to be in 'solidarity' with the strikers. The military mobilisation resulted in the wounding of over thirty people but both the government and the strikers 'adopted a more restrained attitude' (Blanco 1973: 668).

In March 1973, Allende's Popular Unity coalition increased their vote in the General Election to 43 per cent, but the Christian Democrats shifted support from Allende to the right-wing National Party (Roxborough *et al* 1977: 286). On 29 June, members of the military supporting *Patria y Libertad* attempted a coup but were easily defeated. Hugo celebrated the fact that workers were becoming more militant and occupying factories as a manifestation of 'popular power'. In August 1973 the *Guardian* reported that a new Cabinet had been formed which included members of the military.

In response the left, including the youth wing of Allende's own Socialist Party, threatened to withdraw support (Ross 1973). The Cabinet reshuffle failed to win back support from the Christian Democrats who proposed a resolution accusing Allende of ignoring the constitution. Those on the right suggested that he was promoting a Cuban style socialist system. In reality the right, increasingly manipulated by the USA, were preparing to oust Allende.

On 23 August, Allende appointed General Pinochet as commander in chief of the armed forces. On 11 September the military, led by Pinochet, mounted a coup. The junta demanded Allende step down by 11 a.m. and told him that a plane would escort him out of the country, he insisted that he would not leave alive. The air force bombed the Presidential Palace and Allende is thought to have committed suicide. Workers occupied factories and resisted but the armed forces largely supported the emerging junta. Later research showed that despite their denials the USA had actively helped plan the coup.

## Hans Bloom leaves the Embassy

Michel Pablo, the former Fourth International leader who had travelled to Chile and worked for the government supporting workers' self-management projects, summed up the conclusions of many on the left, noting the 'overwhelming majority of the militants, and the masses as a whole expected the coup. But few of them expected such savage repression as that which eventually took place' (Raptis 1974: 89). Lavishly supported by the USA, coup leader General Pinochet was to rule for seventeen years until 1990. During this time it is estimated that eighty thousand individuals were imprisoned for political reasons and over three thousand murdered (Bethell 1993: 178). The worst atrocities occurred in the days after the coup and foreign leftists, like Hugo, were high on the list of those targeted. Peter Camejo feared for Hugo:

> I visited him in Chile and remember my fear for his life when I heard of the military coup against Allende […] A close friend of mine was killed the day of the coup, the leader of a group of Brazilians called 'Grupo Grande'. He could have fled but he waited for his wife at home. The police arrested him and killed him that night (Camejo 2010: 161).

All foreigners had been requested to report to their nearest police station, Hugo knew that it would have been suicide for him to have done so. When the police came to his home to look for him he had already left, rescued by the Swedish Ambassador Harald Edelstam who drove him to the Embassy in his diplomatic car. Edelstam is thought to have saved dozens of people from being killed at the time of the coup. Hugo knew Edelstam because his daughter Carmen went to school with the Ambassador's daughter (Interview August 2018 with Oscar Blanco Berglund). Because there was no asylum treaty between Chile and Sweden, Hugo had to travel via the Mexican Embassy. Edelstam insisted that Hugo shave and dress 'like a respectable gentleman', disguising him as Hans Bloom, a consultant to the Swedish Embassy, so he could pass through the police lines to the safety of the Mexican Ambassador's residence (Blanco 2018a: 136).

Hugo and other escapees were taken by embassy cars to the airport, flying to Sweden via Mexico. He noted this was his seventh cat's life. He was helped by the fact that the head of the police archive had set fire to the records when the coup occurred. Also, the coup leaders were looking for foreigners who had supported Allende; as Hugo was critical of Allende, he did not appear on the lists.

The lesson of Chile was that democracy can be skin deep, Chile had been widely described as the most stable and prosperous Latin American state, immune from the repression and military regimes that plagued the rest of the region. A democratic challenge to capitalism in Latin America, especially in the years of the Cold War, was a challenge too far and the alternative was drowned in blood. The exception proved the rule; as Hugo has consistently noted, capitalism will, if it needs to, use violence to defend privilege; a rule just as relevant in the twenty-first century as in 1973.

Hugo was to live in Sweden until 1975 when he returned to Peru, only to be deported once again. The tragedy in Chile was to reinforce many of his political perspectives but his experience in Sweden was equally if not more significant. He learned Swedish and maintained strong connections with the country after the eventual end of his European exile. Sweden had introduced a measure of social democracy without the threat of a coup or destabilisation by the right. It also had a section of the Fourth International who gave Hugo material and moral support.

Andrés Gonzalez (standing with the checked shirt) was the President of the La Convención and Lares Peasant Union who Hugo met in jail and through whom Hugo joined the struggle for land. To his left is Humberto Carazas and next to him is Leonidas Carpio. The others are also peasant leaders from diverse unions in La Convención and Lares involved in the fight for land reform. This photo was taken in the 1960s.

Hugo around the time of his 80th birthday, 2014.

Hugo is with Zaragoza, Gerardo Carpio´s wife. When the men, including her husband, were imprisoned, their wives went on hunger strike. Even when their husbands were freed, they persisted, as the strike was for all land reform prisoners. She explained this to journalists, and then, lifting her left fist, yelled "Tierra o Muerte!, Venceremos!" Taken around the time of his 80th birthday, 2014.

Hugo is with Denise Carpio, the granddaughter of Leonidas Carpio who was involved with Hugo in the struggles in La Convención and Lares. Today Denise campaigns against the building of Hydroelectric dams on the Marañon river. This was a wonderful discovery for Hugo as he is involved in the fight to save water. Taken around the time of his 80th birthday, 2014.

Taken on Hugo's 80th birthday in Marunara, where the Convención and Lares Peasant Union organized a march in his honour. Hugo refused to be honoured alone and looked for every one of his comrades, inviting them to the march and celebration.

Hugo taken around the time of his 80th birthday, 2014.

Hugo with his children – from left to right Maria, Oscar, Bruno, Hugo, Marco, and Carmen, 2004.

Hugo in Cusco by the famous Inca wall, during the Into Raymi, 21 June 2014.

# 6

# Political Life 1973-1992

'The projects of the left continued to be crushed by the majority, the servants of the oppressors.' Hugo Blanco (2018a: 17).

After his release in December 1970 Hugo had shuttled from Peru to Mexico, Mexico to Argentina, Argentina to Chile, witnessed a bloody coup and spent many months in jail. After this period of crisis and instability, exile to Sweden gave him a period of relative calm and ended the threat of repression. Nonetheless, he was eager to return to Peru and engage in political struggle. Back in Peru, his political activities ranged from running for the Presidency to aiding land occupations. This chapter looks at Hugo's political life between 1973 and 1992.

## The fight against repression

Inger Wahlöö wrote in the daily newspaper *Expressen* on 6 November, 'Hugo Blanco's life is safe at last. He has spent his first night in the only country that offered him asylum – Sweden.' (Anon 1973: 1327). Arriving in Stockholm, Hugo's main priority was to work against the repression both in Chile and increasingly across Latin America. Daily life in Sweden involved family commitments and he worked as a language teacher. He spoke at meetings both in Sweden and other parts of Europe raising awareness of the brutality of the Pinochet regime. However, he was keen to return to Peru at the earliest opportunity.

His eldest daughter Carmen, who had lived with him in Chile, moved to Sweden.

She also came from Cusco to Sweden in 1975 to be closer to her father, but at that time they did not live together, she in Stockholm and he in Uppsala. Carmen has lived in Sweden since that time when she was 15 years old, with frequent visits to Peru. She has two daughters with Göran Nordling, also a teacher, Paloma and Sissela. Sissela is a former leader of the Feminist Party and at present an incumbent candidate for the municipal elections in Stockholm. (Comment from Gunilla Berglund August 2018)

While his family connections with Sweden are strong, Hugo remained concerned with events in Peru rather than European politics. Interviewed in 1974, Hugo suggested that while he saw no hope of transforming the Peruvian regime into a worker's state, there was a danger of it being replaced by something far worse:

With respect to the coup in Chile: This event shifted the relationship of forces in South America against the masses. One of its consequences was the creation of the bloc of pro-imperialist strong governments – Chile, Brazil, Bolivia, and Uruguay. This bloc represents an attack not only on the people of those four countries but also poses a grave threat to the people of the other South American nations.

From a distance it is difficult to estimate how close Peru is to a reactionary coup. My comrades of the FIR [*Frente de Izquierda Revolucionaria* – Front of the Revolutionary Left] point out in the organization's paper, *Palabra Socialista*, that such a danger exists, although only in a latent form. (Blanco 1974: 990-991)

Hugo was now working as an assistant to a Spanish teacher in Sandöskolan, an auxiliary school in Kramfors to the north of Härnösand. Living in this town in Northern Sweden, he was undergoing treatment for back problems caused by imprisonment and beatings (Anon 1974: 1435).

## Hector does not understand

Hugo had continued to make efforts to return to Peru, appealing to the country's Swedish ambassador to support his return. In October 1974 the issue of Hugo's return and the contradictory approaches of the left to the government that had exiled him were presented dramatically when the Swedish newspaper *Dagens Nyheter* arranged a debate between him and Héctor Béjar. Béjar, a Peruvian guerrilla, had been released in 1970 at the same time as Hugo. In contrast to Hugo, he had pledged his support to the reformist military regime and was visiting Sweden to learn more about the trade union movement in the country. Béjar, at the time, was working for the Peruvian government advising on social mobilisation.

The debate was unproductive. Béjar argued that the Peruvian government was anti-imperialist and deserved Hugo's support. Hugo asked why, if this was the case, he and other Peruvian leftists remained exiled by Velasco's government:

It seems as if Héctor did not understand my question and its intent. In exile here is Rolando Breña, the Peruvian student leader. The students did not choose him from among the oligarchy. Nor was this the case for the leader of the teachers' strike or of the mine workers, for Naturi Cuentas, or Gustavo Rui de Sommo Cursos, who took part in the Arequipa strike.

These comrades do not belong to the oligarchy; they took part in the workers struggle. They have been deported. No law in my country authorizes such deportations. Has this illegal situation been ended yet? (Anon 1974: 1435).

Hugo met his partner Gunilla in 1975. Gunilla, while politically active, was not a member of the Fourth International then but, at the time, a group closer to Maoism. The *Svenska Clartéförbundet* was a student socialist group linked in the 1970s to the Communist League (Marxist Leninist). Gunilla subsequently became a Trotskyist. She was with Hugo during more dramatic years between 1975 and 1983. Although they separated in 1983, with Gunilla returning to Sweden, they seemed to have remained on good terms since. Gunilla is a psychologist,

and until recently a lecturer in Stockholm University, the Institution of Psychology. She met Hugo in early 1975 when she was a guest during a ski holiday with Hugo's students from Sandöskolan in the very north of Sweden. This stay was followed by Hugo´s coming to Uppsala to live with her. They lived together in Uppsala, Lima and Stockholm on and off until 1983. They have two children Maria and Oscar. (Comment from Gunilla Berglund August 2018)

During 1975 Hugo was aware that the likelihood of a coup in Peru was increasing. The right were organising against the government, including bomb attacks on ministers and the shooting of a journalist. As in Chile, attempts were being made to disrupt the economy so as to provoke unrest, including arson attacks on the state-owned Minero Peru, a cotton warehouse and state food distributor. As in Chile, Hugo argued that the left need to mobilize workers and oppose any coup; the state, by repressing the workers, made its own removal more likely.

In August 1975 the *New York Times* reported that 'Juan Velasco was replaced by General Francisco Morales-Bermúdez 'who is widely considered a more conservative and pragmatic leader' (Hofman 1975: 1). The coup, known as El Tacnazo, began with a military takeover of the town of Tacna, where Hugo had been tried in the 1960s (Cheyre 2013: 20). Velasco had become severely ill and the Peruvian economy was in crisis. However, while the right gained control, there was no repeat of the kind of repression seen in Chile. Rather than a military regime replacing a democratically elected and popular government, and in doing so needing huge forces of violence, this was a shift in power from one general to another, a shift to the right, but a less radical shift than seen in Chile.

The coup was apparently bloodless, but the new President General Francisco Morales-Bermúdez, also affected by political challenges and economic crisis, promised a transition back to democracy. The promise of democracy was to allow Hugo Blanco to return to Peru, but both the process of democratisation and Hugo's return were to be complex and interrupted processes.

## Return to Peru

Much of 1975 was taken up with plans for Hugo to undertake a speaking tour of the USA, at the invitation of the US Committee for Justice to Latin American Political Prisoners (USLA). Hugo's visa was denied, with the authorities citing his communist beliefs and support for 'terrorism'. However, he did briefly make it to the USA; the plane he was travelling on returning to Peru had engine difficulties and was forced to land in Miami. Asked why his visa had been refused, he blamed Henry Kissinger, the US Secretary of State:

> Kissinger is afraid that I will speak on the things yankee imperialism is doing in Latin America – many of them directed by Kissinger himself. He knows I've been in Peru, I've been in Argentina, I've been in Chile, and I know firsthand what the United States is doing in those countries. Kissinger doesn't want me coming here to tell the North American people about it. (Blanco 1975b: 1490).

However, he was going back to Peru for the first time since 1971. Bermúdez had announced an amnesty for all of those, both on the left and the right, who had been deported:

> The new government says it recognizes the freedom to criticize. Well, I am going to exercise that right.
> The new government also says that, although it recognizes freedom of criticism and has granted amnesty, it will be severe with those who try to halt the revolutionary process. You can accuse me of anything else, but certainly not of trying to halt the revolutionary process! (Blanco 1975b: 1490).

While the coup had moved the junta to the right, and in subsequent years they would become more beholden to the International Monetary Fund, they were still insisting that their regime was promoting a process of revolution. The regime insisted that the left, workers and peasants should only be part of official pro-government networks and criticised those like Hugo who refused to join them.

Back in Peru, Hugo was shadowed by police officers when he travelled, however 'everywhere the threat of uniforms was drowned in flowers and embraces' as people came to greet him. He returned to La Convención for the first time since his arrest in 1963:

'Kausachun!' Long live Hugo Blanco, in the peasants' language, Quechua. From the outskirts of the village to the peasants' meeting place in the center of Quiabamha, the people crowded along behind the truck. It was the middle of the night, but the people wanted to hear Blanco speak. They wanted to have him sit at their tables and dance the *huayno* with them.

Two hours' sleep on a cold dirt floor before the next day's meetings and problems. (Anon 1976a: 46)

The 'problems' referred to occurred because the *campesinos* were divided. Some supported the land reform of the military government; others were supportive of Hugo, who criticised Velasco's reforms as inadequate and bureaucratic. When the air became thick with stone throwing and argument at a rally he was addressing, Hugo noted with disappointment, 'What a tragedy!'. Nonetheless tensions were dispersed with the singing of a traditional *huayno*, a song composed in La Frontón prison by a comrade, including the words 'the farmers of today and tomorrow will never forget Hugo Blanco' (Anon 1976a: 46).

Hugo travelled across Peru promoting indigenous, trade union and other social movement struggles, as a member of the Socialist Workers Party (*Partido Socialista de los Trabajadores*), a section of the Fourth International. A report by a Swedish journalist covered his visit to the shanty town known as Kilometre 14:

'It's him. Don't you see, it's him. That's Hugo Blanco!' When Hugo Blanco entered the market place, the news of his coming had preceded him.

The shantytown in the desert had no name. Those who live here usually call it 'Kilometer 14,' after its distance from Lima.

Hugo Blanco had been there only once before. But slogans in big letters on walls remained from his visit: 'Hugo Blanco, the indefatigable defender of the peasants,' the signs said. 'Hugo Blanco, champion of the working class.' 'Welcome, Hugo Blanco!' (Holmberg 1976: 441)

During the 1980s and early 1990s, the Maoist Shining Path were to plunge Peru into a brutal war; the Maoists targeted other currents on the left. An early indication of the coming storm was when a Maoist group prevented Hugo from speaking at the San Marco University in Lima on 2 April. He spoke at another university meeting on 8 April, but the Maoists physically attacked members of the audience. Hugo denounced the 'reactionary foreign policy being followed by Peking'; US President Richard Nixon had travelled to China and met Mao in 1972. Hugo also criticised the Maoist theory that in countries like Peru 'the national bourgeoisie is revolutionary' (Anon 1976b: 951). Peru's divided Maoists had little impact during the 1970s.

## Deportations, strikes, elections

On 3 July 1976, Hugo was arrested by the PIP, at his brother's home in Cusco, and deported to Sweden two days later. This was part of a general round up by the regime, as protests against economic austerity were growing in the country. Both left and right continued to organise. On 1 July mass demonstrations had swept through the shanty towns surrounding Lima calling for an end to military rule and wage increases. Hugo was arrested along with three hundred other left activists, some of whom were also deported. The authorities said that they had acted against Hugo because of his support for a strike at Manufacturas Nylon S.A. near Lima. Put on a plane to Madrid, he returned to Sweden (White 1976: 1092).

Events were moving in Peru and Hugo's new exile was to be relatively brief. The military regime, faced with economic and political crisis, agreed to make a transition to democracy in two steps. A Constitutional Assembly was to be elected in 1978, with Presidential elections, the first since the 1960s, in 1980. The left had started to organise, and attempts were made to present a united list of candidates for the Assembly. FOCEP [*Frente Obrero, Campesino, Estudiantil, y Popular* – Workers, Peasants, Students, and Popular Front] was formed with the support of a variety of political parties on the left, including Hugo's Socialist Workers Party. Hugo was allowed to return to Peru in April 1978. Keen to put his energy into FOCEP's election campaign he noted that any left victory would lead to a response from the right,

in the crisis situation that prevails, the people will certainly utilize every increase in human rights to improve their situation. But when the class struggle becomes too sharp, repression will increase. (Anon 1978d: 500-501).

And the repression came once again; in response to a television interview where Hugo had supported a General Strike, he was arrested. Martial law was proclaimed and the constituent assembly elections due to be held in June were postponed. Gunilla Berglund told journalists that at 4.30 a.m., ten members of the PIP had come to their home in Lima, informed Hugo that the minister of the interior wished to speak to him, and placed him in detention (Anon 1978a: 628). Hugo, despite being a leading election candidate, was deported along with other left-wing candidates including:

Genaro Ledesma Izquieta of FOCEP, a well-known labor attorney; Ricardo Napurf, also of FOCEP, a central leader of the Partido Obrero Marxista Revolucionario (Revolutionary Marxist Workers Party); Ricardo Diaz Chavez, an attorney for the miners' union and a candidate of the Democratic People's Union (UDP); Ricardo Letts Colmenares of the UDP, an editor of the weekly magazine Marka; and Javier Diez Canseco, UDP candidate and member of the editorial board of the weekly *Amauta*. (Anon 1978b: 661)

All were taken to Argentina, a choice that put their lives in danger. Argentina continued to be ruled by a right-wing junta with an appalling human rights record, noted like Chile for executing suspected opponents without trial. Operation Condor, a US backed plan to murder leftists, coordinated by the different right-wing regimes in Latin America, was in existence at the time. In 2017, General Bermúdez, then aged 95, was found guilty of human rights abuse as a result of Condor (Anon 2017). USLA observed 'Until Hugo Blanco and Ricardo Diaz Chavez − and any of the other Peruvians who may wish to − have been allowed to leave Argentina safely they are not out of danger from right-wing death squads' (Anon 1978c: 693). Hugo was imprisoned in an army barracks but was eventually allowed to fly back to Sweden, where he was greeted by his eldest daughter Carmen at Stockholm Airport (Murphy 1978a: 756).

When the election was called, FOCEP campaigned strongly as a coalition united on basic principles, including support for the struggles of working people, and opposition to the military government and the 'bourgeois parties' such as the Christian Democrats. (Murphy 1978b: 788-789). While the centre and right parties won the most votes, the FOCEP were the strongest force on the left and received over 11 per cent of the vote, which was enough to elect Hugo Blanco. The rest of the left was divided between the Revolutionary Socialist Party (PSR) on 5.9 per cent which supported the left of the military regime, the Communist Party with 5.7 per cent, the Democratic People's Union (UDP) which included some Maoists and Communist Party dissidents and received 4.2 per cent, and a number of smaller groups. In total, candidates claiming to be on the left received 27 per cent of the vote (Murphy 1978b: 788). The left was growing but very divided, however with a system of proportional representation, the various groups were able to elect members of the Assembly. With the FOCEP coming third across the country, Hugo had won a place.

Despite his election victory the authorities refused to allow Hugo back in the country, so he undertook a speaking tour in Europe denouncing his continuing exile. 1978 saw a wave of strikes, land occupations and protests across Peru. Eventually the authorities allowed him to return. He participated in both electoral politics and grassroots activism, supporting workers and peasants. His already strong status was enhanced by regular television appearances and Lima weekly magazine *Amauta* named Hugo as 'man of the year' in 1978 (Anon 1979: 13).

APRA, once a radical party, was perceived as the only force that could prevent the divided but radical left, propelled by increasingly confident social movements representing workers, indigenous and especially those dwelling in the vast shanty towns around Lima, from taking power:

> The scene at the opening of the constituent assembly captured the mood in Peru today. As Hugo Blanco was sworn in as an Assembly deputy, striking school teachers battled police and Aprista thugs in the streets surrounding the Legislative Palace. Inside, as wafts of tear gas drifted through the galleries, Blanco took the oath by raising his fist and shouting: 'For the working class, for the world socialist revolution, for the blood that was shed this morning – yes, I swear.' (Bollinger 1978: 45)

The Constituent Assembly, Peru's tenth, replaced the constitution of the 1930s. There were some positive aspects to the new constitution, including the right of illiterate citizens to vote. Around half of the campesinos in the Andes could not read, so the literacy requirement had prevented them from voting. This reform, long demanded by the left, increased access to the system,

Each party's symbol appeared on the ballot so those who could not read could mark their choice: a star for APRA, a banner for the United Left, a shovel for the Popular Action Party, and so forth. (Starn 1999: 231).

With the election of President Carter, a Democrat who replaced more right-wing Republicans, Hugo was able to finally undertake his speaking tour of the USA, denouncing 'Yankee imperialism as the vanguard for the crushing of human rights in our countries' in forty-eight US cities to 10,000 people (Blanco 2018a: 16). He spent six months between 1977 and 1978 touring the US with his partner Gunilla and their daughter Maria:

> It was a loophole that allowed it. US had created a loophole to enable Alexander Solzhenitsyn to come. But the loophole was used by US supporters to get Hugo a visa. In light of Carter's concern for human rights, I believe the speaking tour's theme was 'Jimmy Carter and human rights in Latin America'. (Interview August 2018 with Oscar Blanco Berglund).

Maria was born in Stockholm in 1977:

> She lived on and off with her father until she was 6. After her parents' separation she went to Peru to see him every second year (as well as her brother Oscar) and as an adult after having her teacher diploma and some experiences of teaching in Sweden she returned to Perú. She works occasionally as a tour leader and lives with her family in Pisaq outside Cusco. She has a daughter, Ronia eight, and a son, Wari two and a half. Her partner is called Benjamin and he comes from Cusco. Maria is passionate about sustainable living, drawing on Andean traditions. (Comment from Gunilla Berglund August 2018)

In August 1979 Hugo travelled to Nicaragua to support the new revolutionary government that had thrown out Somoza's US backed dictatorship. He celebrated the revolution and argued that the masses should be armed to resist any attempt to restore the right (Blanco 1979).

In 1980, he ran for Peruvian President as the Revolutionary Workers Party (PRT) candidate, representing the Fourth International. His dynamic campaign drew huge crowds and made good use of television appearances. Belaúnde, who had been deposed by the 1968 coup, was elected on a right-wing platform with 44 per cent, APRA came second with 27 per cent and Hugo, the highest scoring left candidate, was fourth with 4 per cent. The

PRT succeeded in electing two Senators and three member of Congress, including Hugo representing a Lima district (Beauvais 1980: 562).

Hugo was to have been the left unity candidate in 1980 as part of the Revolutionary Left Alliance, but this fell apart. Standing for the PRT for the Presidency, Hugo had helped divide the left vote. The PRT was also slow to join the United Left (IU), which became a major force, electing a Mayor in Lima and scaring the Peruvian establishment. Hugo, interviewed in 1984, admitted that under his leadership the PRT had made mistakes:

> There are two key things we have to look at. One is the question of unity and of the united front, which is central to the revolution. The other is the question of political line, of clarity about upholding working-class political independence. The essential question is how to combine these two things in the concrete situation we face. We now feel that we underestimated the need for unity and the sentiment in favor of unity among the masses and that we overemphasized, or even fetishized, our own doctrinal purity.
>
> As a result of this, we did not fight energetically enough to unify the FOCEP and the UDP, which were two powerful fronts that arose in the period when the Morales Bermudez government was coming to an end. Later, we were unable to consolidate and maintain the ARI as a left front led by revolutionaries, And we did not join the United Left when it was formed. As a result, we have now been pushed to the sidelines in the consciousness of the masses.
>
> We made a big error. We should have paid more attention to concrete actions and deeds than to formal declarations and nit-picking over words. Such an attitude led us into a kind of sectarianism that isolated us. (Blanco 1984: 155-156)

The PRT had rejected one left unity project because it included the group Socialist Political Action, 'which only had four members!' noted Hugo observing that such 'sectarian scruples have done us great harm.' (Blanco 1984: 156)

Hugo, reflecting on his parliamentary experience also observed 'I should have refused to be a candidate for Lima'; instead, he felt, he should have sought election in Cusco 'close to the grassroots and obeyed their orders' (Blanco 2014a: 283). However his time in Congress and later in the Senate saw him defending workers and indigenous people with his customary energy. He noted he was beaten up by the police on numerous occasions supporting protest marches, and was hospitalised at one point due to a head injury (Blanco 2018a: 17).

## From congress to coffee sales

During this time his second son, Oscar was born:

> Oscar Blanco Berglund was born in 1982 in Stockholm. He visited Peru every other year as a child and has lived there for shorter periods. Since 2005 he lives in England with his wife Kelly and their children, Gabriel (10) and Amelie (6). Oscar is an academic, working at the University of Bristol and he researches anti-austerity social movements and parties and teaches international political economy and public policy. (Comment from Gunilla Berglund August 2018)

In 1983 Hugo was suspended from Congress for three months, after accusing General Roberto Clemente Noel of genocide. Later, a Peruvian Truth Commission found that Noel had been guilty of extra-judicial killings and torture in the Ayacucho region. Noel's assault on the indigenous was part of the authorities' flawed attempt to combat Shining Path's Maoist insurgency (Blanco 2018a: 17). Having lost his place in Congress, Hugo became a coffee vendor in Lima.

> One day a journalist from one of the local dailies asked me if I was not embarrassed to sell coffee on the street. 'Look,' I said, 'just two blocks away, other congressmen dressed in expensive suits and ties are selling out the country and they don't seem to be bothered by it. So why should I be embarrassed by earning a living in an honest manner?' (Olivera 2011).

After the end of his term in 1985, having entered the United Left coalition, he did not seek re-election to congress and instead devoted himself to the role of leader of the Campesino Confederation of Peru (CCP). He moved to the province of Puno, which is near Cusco, where the *campesinos* were occupying cooperatives created by Velasco's military government. While Velasco had broken the power of the *gamonales*, his land reform was often bureaucratic and gave officials power over the *campesinos*. Hugo proudly noted that he participated in struggles to recover 1,250,000 hectares of land for local communities (Blanco 2018a: 17). He then travelled to the Piura region on the coast of Peru, to support the *ronda campesinas*. The *rondas* were self-defence groups established by the *campesinos* to prevent the theft of livestock and to provide community policing as an alternative to the often corrupt and racist official forces of law and order (Starn 1999).

Around this time in the mid–1980s, Hugo lost an eighth cat's life – but uniquely this had nothing to do with repression or political violence. A train to Cusco was derailed and overturned; Hugo, in severe pain walked to the police station to report the accident and took a taxi to his brother Oscar's house. Oscar then took him to a different hospital to most of the injured. Finding him missing, other passengers in hospital who knew Hugo had been on their train thought he had been killed. His death was reported on television, but he was able to let people know that this was false news (Interview July 2018).

In 1984, the Unified Mariátegui Party (PUM) was founded and provided a means of uniting a number of far-left parties. The PUM participated in both electoral politics and social movement struggles, they were strongly involved in the campesino movement and urban self-organisation networks (Roberts 1998: 228-229). In 1990 Hugo was elected as a Senator on a PUM ticket, as part of the United Left. He contributed his salary as a senator to pay for a secretary for the CCP, however progress through conventional political channels was largely thwarted.

In 1989 he came close to being killed in the rainforest region of Ucayali. Striking *campesinos* were blocking roads in desperate protest at the low prices they received for their crops, the effects of soaring interest rates on the development loans they received, and to gain land reform. The feared anti-terrorist police attacked, killing many demonstrators, Hugo was arrested and beaten. He was kicked in the abdomen and feared that he would be killed, 'disappeared' like so many others.

> Seeing at the time, Peru was leading the league tables of disappearances globally, it is reasonable to think that this was the intention. The saving of his life was thanks to reports that he was captured by the army quickly spreading and globally, allowing a swift campaign for his release and making it impossible to 'disappear' him. (Interview August 2018 with Oscar Blanco Berglund).

In Pucallpa, where the massacre had occurred, Hugo was put on trial accused of terrorism. He summed up his defence speech with the words, 'I long for the day when the Peruvian courts stop putting the victims, the survivors of the massacres on trial; and for the day when they are replaced by the instigators and authors' (Blanco 2018a: 85). However once again international solidarity provided the pressure necessary to free him.

## The environmentalism of the people

After joining the Senate's Environmental Commission in the early 1990s Hugo visited communities affected by mining (Blanco 2008a: 22). His activism and writings contributed to the emergence of environmental justice movements, and later to developing the concept of ecosocialism. His 1991 essay 'The Environmentalism of the People', reprinted and translated into English in the US socialist journal *Against the Current*, contrasted the elitist approach of some conservationists with the environmental concerns of poorer communities, noting that the cloud forests 'have been inhabited for thousands of years by people who know how to coexist with, and be part of, their environment'. He suggested that the NGOs were often false friends of the environment, blaming peasants and street vendors for damage instead of the giant corporations:

> Without doubt, some environmentalists don't want to accuse these big polluters of the environment. Whom do they blame instead? The street vendors who litter the area where they sell, or the bus driver, or the peasant who cuts down a tree in order to celebrate with the 'yunsa' in the carnival.
>
> Of course we are not in favor of the children killing the birds in the parks or of someone stepping on the tail of the cat that belongs to one of the ladies of Miraflores. But there is no comparison between these actions and the actions of those that export animals by the hundreds from the jungle or with the foreign-owned monopoly company 'Michael and Sarfati' that kills hundreds of vicunas for their wool.
>
> These false environmentalists, some from Non-Governmental Organizations, have as their real objective to cover up for the real despoilers of the environment. For that reason they are anti-environmentalists. (Blanco 1993).

A particular environmental issue that concerned him in 1992 was the fate of the anchovy. As part of a Senate investigation he visited the anchovy fishers and found that they had been forced by their bosses, with declining anchovy stocks, to catch the younger fish, the *peladilla*. The *peladilla* is very slippery, making fishing dangerous, and lives had been lost; catching this fish also accelerates the decline in numbers. Alerted by Maria Elena Foronda of the environmental group Natura, he also investigated sea pollution.

However, within days Fujimori had declared his self-coup, Hugo had to flee the country and Maria was imprisoned on false charges. Hugo was aware that a desire for short term profit led to corruption, authoritarianism and environmental devastation (Blanco 2018a: 161). During the 1980s and 1990s Peruvian politics was dominated by the war between the authorities and the Maoist Shining Path. This killed tens of thousands and devastated the social movements on the left that Hugo supported.

## Shining Path

It started in a small but bizarre way. The anthropologist Carlos Iván Degregori has told and retold the story:

> On the night of May 17 1980, the eve of Peru's first presidential elections in 17 years, a group of youths broke into the town hall in the small Andean town of Chuschi. They took ballot boxes and voting lists, and burned them in the town plaza. The incident was lost in the avalanche of election news. Over the following months, while the press reported the theft of dynamite from a few mines, isolated bombs began to go off here and there. No one paid much attention until the end of that year, when the situation acquired a folkloric if sinister dimension: Early risers in Lima began to find dead dogs hung from traffic lights and lamp posts. They were adorned with signs that read, 'Deng Xiao Ping, Son of a Bitch.' (Degregori 1992)

The Communist Party of Peru, known commonly as Shining Path, had begun its 'peoples war'. Hugo Blanco compared Shining Path with Pol Pot's Khmer Rouge in Cambodia, observing 'Sendero exhibits many of the most negative aspects of Maoism in its most sectarian period' (Blanco 1984: 154). He stated that the 'fundamental reason for the emergence of Sendero Luminoso – whose full name is Partido Comunista del Perú – Sendero Luminoso' was the desperate 'poverty of the peasants in Ayacucho, Huancavelica, and Apurimac, – along with the failure of the rest of the left to present an alternative to the present conditions' (Blanco 1984: 154).

During the 1960s, conflict between Mao's China and the Soviet Union led pro-Chinese members to leave the official Communist Parties and set up their own anti-revisionist organisations. Mao's 1972 détente with US President Nixon confused things further, with some Maoist groups rejecting China and advocating loyalty to Albania's hard-line leader Enver Hoxha (Elbaum 2018: 236-237). Maoism potentially had a number of attractions. Mao had undertaken a successful revolution, indicating strategic sense, and in a country like Peru with many impoverished *campesinos*, his emphasis on the leading role of the peasantry was also appealing.

Shining Path was led by a professor of philosophy, Abimael Guzmán, better known as Chairman Gonzalo, who taught at San Cristóbal of Huamanga National University in Ayacucho. He joined the Peruvian Communist Party-Red Flag (PCP-BR), the pro-Chinese group that had left the PCP, becoming a leader of its Ayacucho regional committee during the 1960s (Degregori 2012: 73). After successive splits, the PCP-SL was formed.

The 1970s were spent in intellectual seclusion with Guzmán and his followers, whose unique area of influence was within the Ayacucho university, developing their political line. Mariátegui, from whom the phrase 'shining path' was taken, was studied obsessively. Guzmán promoted a cult of personality based upon strict adherence to his system of thought. By the late 1970s, preparations were made for the peoples' war. Shining Path took little part in the social unrest that had swept through Peru in the late 1970s and showed no interest in the complex electoral politics of the left. The isolation and esoteric nature of their message meant that they too were ignored by both the left and the Peruvian authorities.

While developing their political line, Shining Path had steadily recruited members, particularly students and teachers. In contrast to the largely Spanish speaking student leftists who had tried to engage in guerrilla wars in imitation of Che in the 1960s, Shining Path's youthful cadres came from the Quechua population. Many of them moved back to the Andes, often as teachers, so a network of militants was patiently constructed (Taylor 2006: 6). Ideological preparation, recruitment and isolation from social struggles allowed Shining Path to build a strong basis for their forthcoming campaign.

Their military campaign, based on a classic strategy derived from Mao, began in 1980. Guzmán promoted the concept of a protracted peoples war based on the tactic of *batir el campo*:

> cleansing the countryside, incendiarising it, removing all the political authorities and landlords, eliminating all functionaries. The rural areas should be thrown into confusion, the land cleansed before we sow and build up revolutionary bases of support. (Guzmán quoted in Taylor 2006: 20)

The aim was to undertake a guerrilla war in rural areas, supplemented by urban warfare, that would eventually surround the cities and destroy the class enemy. The killing of unjust landlords and land occupations raised support from many *campesinos*. The Peruvian state was still weak in much of the Andes, and the authorities in the late 1970s and late 1980s were focused on existing social movements, so Shining Path was able to act at first with little or no official military response.

The peasants in areas under Shining Path control were only allowed to produce what they could consume; any surplus was forbidden:

> Sendero claims that this is to sabotage the Belaúnde government. But considering the minuscule percentage of the gross domestic product that these harvests make up, obviously this has no effect on the regime.
>
> It has a terrible effect, however, on the peasants themselves. When they are unable to sell part of their crop, they cannot buy matches or any other commodity they need but do not produce themselves. The result is they are being forced down to a bare subsistence level. (Blanco 1984: 154)

Peasant leaders were often killed and replaced with Shining Path members, *campesino* self-organisation was seen as harmful to the party's revolutionary ambitions. Shining Path were able to dominate large areas of the countryside. However, their inflexible approach meant that such support diminished over time. As the conflict continued, Shining Path were able to spread to urban areas, particularly the shanty towns that surrounded cities such as Lima. They targeted any other group on the left, killing many members of socialist organisations and social movements. Most notoriously María Elena Moyano, the left wing and feminist deputy mayor of the Villa El Salvador shanty town outside Lima, was machine gunned to death. The Shining Path cadres then proceeded to blow her body up with dynamite (Poole and Rénique 1992: 92).

Successive Peruvian presidents, noting Mao's principle that the peasants act as the sea that shelters the guerrillas who were the fish, launched a dirty war against the *campesinos*. Any supposed disloyalty on the part of *campesinos* was punished by Shining Path and any perceived support for Shining Path was met by retribution from the state. It is estimated between 1980 and 1999 nearly seventy thousand people, mostly *campesinos,* were killed (Degregori 2012: 3). There were other crimes:

> In the Fujimori period in Peru, a program of forced sterilization was developed – directed mostly at native Quechua women – called the 'Public Health Plan'. It was principally financed with US$36 million from the US Agency for International Development (USAID) and United Nations Population Fund (UNFPA). Between 1995 and 2000, a total of 331,600 women were sterilized – some of whom died as a result of the operation – while 25,590 men suffered vasectomies. Doctors and nurses were fired if they failed to meet their sterilization quotas. The plan was implemented against rural people and those in marginal urban areas. (Blanco 2014b: 2)

Shining Path were diminished by the capture of Guzmán in September 1992 (Hunefeldt 2004: 258).   The war continued, involving a second guerrilla force, the MRTA, but petered out by 2000. In 2018 Shining Path, with a few remaining members fighting in the *selva,* has attempted to create a legal political party, *El Movimiento por la Amnistía y los Derechos Fundamentales* (Movadef) campaigning for an amnesty and the release of Guzmán (Bel 2017).

In 1992 Hugo was forced once again in to exile. Both the Shining Path and Peru's internal security services placed him on death lists, as part of the dirty war, so he escaped to Mexico. The Mexican experience, where he met the Zapatistas, was to transform his outlook, but a commitment to environmental concerns was now a major part of his conscious political philosophy. The Zapatistas stress the need not to take power from the state, either via elections or armed struggle, but instead to create their own power by building alternative institutions.

# With the Zapatistas 1992-2002

There are indigenous struggles on all continents against the racist and colonial mentality and politics that defend the capitalist system. What's been happening for twenty-three years in Chiapas, Mexico, in the Zapatista zone, makes me optimistic. I hear what the Zapatistas say: 'Please don't copy us. Everyone in their place and in their time will know how it's done.' Hugo Blanco (Hamilton 2017)

Hugo moved to Mexico and came into contact with the Zapatistas, whose radicalism reshaped his political thinking. Returning to Peru in 1997 he increasingly engaged with ecological concerns and indigenous politics.

## Zapatista lives!

On 5 April 1992 the Peruvian President Fujimori declared his self-coup, sent tanks to close down Congress and attempted to imprison political opponents, including the previous APRA president Alan Garcia, who escaped to Colombia (Conaghan 2005: 28). Hugo moved to Mexico,

> I left Peru during the Fujimori dictatorship. I found out that I was sentenced to death by the National Intelligence Service, headed by the nefarious Vladimiro Montesinos (now a prisoner) and also sentenced to death by the Sendero Luminoso sect.
>
> I got in touch with the Mexican comrades. I did not do political work. I visited several places in the country as a seller of Peruvian and Mexican handicrafts at fairs. (Interview August 2018)

While he was, perhaps uniquely, not doing political work, he stated that he was 'fortunate to be there when the Zapatista rebellion exploded' (Blanco 2008a: 22).

The Zapatistas, who at the time were completely unknown, launched an uprising in January 1994 in the southern Mexican state of Chiapas. The

Zapatista Army of National Liberation (EZLN) occupied the city of San Cristóbal de las Casas along with six other towns, on the day that the North American Free Trade Agreement (NAFTA) was due to come into effect. The free trade agreement between Mexico, Canada and USA threatened the communal land ownership of the indigenous people of Chiapas. The masked, pipe smoking and mysterious Subcomandante Marcos was their most emblematic symbol. Although the Zapatistas retreated from the towns they were occupying, they made their mark (Weinberg 2002).

By 1990s the left, not only in Peru but globally, was confused, dismayed and generally in retreat. The collapse of the Soviet Union and the advance of free market values suggested to many that socialism was dead, and the only revolution would be in retail. The Zapatistas, however, knew that many communities were oppressed and organised for liberation.

Still active in 2018 as I write, they emphasise the construction of indigenous institutions independent from the state, strongly promoting self-government. While building local community structures they have sought to use the media including, in 1994, the then infant world wide web, to build international support.

They called international gatherings to unite revolutionaries from a wide spectrum of traditions to meet and discuss how to challenge global capitalism. While Hugo Blanco lived south of Mexico City, far from Chiapas, he was eager to learn more about their approach to political transformation. His visits to the Zapatistas suggested to him that self-government was viable option:

> The Zapatistas have three levels of government: the community, the municipality, and the region. Many thousands of indigenous people govern themselves democratically with the principle of 'lead by obeying'. The people choose a group of women and men as governors, but they don't choose a president or a secretary general; all those chosen have the same rank. After a period of time they change out everyone, there's no reelection, so everyone is at the head and there's no indispensable person. When there's a very important question, they convene a general assembly so that the collective decides. (Hamilton 2017)

Evolving partly from Maoism, based amongst the indigenous and committed to armed struggle, the Zapatistas shared some apparent features with the followers of Abimael Guzmán, but were radically different (Harvey 1995). Both have combined an emphasis on the revolutionary potential of the indigenous with reference to Marx, but for the Zapatistas this has meant putting the community in control, rather than controlling the community as with Shining Path. In contrast to earlier manifestations of the armed Latin American left, the Zapatistas rejected the need for a Leninist Party or form of hierarchical leadership, instead embracing an autonomist or perhaps anarchist perspective.

Hugo Blanco has argued 'I am a Zapatista. I do not believe in struggling to take power, but to build it', showing some contrast with both his earlier Leninism and his participation in electoral politics (Weinberg 2009). His son Oscar told me that contact with Zapatistas also led to his 'green radicalisation'. Indeed Hugo noted, 'They are ecologists; they eat the food they grow themselves, and they don't use agrochemicals or GMOs'. (Saul 2015). Certainly there is a change in his words between the Leninist tone in the twentieth century and a more radically ecological and indigenous language used in the twenty first. Nonetheless, a green strand has been apparent from Hugo's early desire to work the land and his participation in the Senate Environmental Committee during the 1990s. Soil conservation has long been his concern. Indeed, writing *Land or Death* while in prison in the 1960s, he noted that Spanish invaders had destroyed the agricultural terraces they found which led to erosion, 'murder[ing] the soil' (Blanco 1977: 28).

Hugo had been close to his brother Oscar, who led a professional career as an agronomist. Oscar sadly died in 1994 of cancer. The brothers shared a passion for plants, soil and ecology:

Oscar was very close to Hugo and his old house, where two of his daughters now live, is still where Hugo stays when he visits Cusco. As an agronomist, Oscar liked to travel to different parts of the countryside and learn from the practices of farmers. He worked at the University of Cusco (Universidad Nacional San Antonio Abad de Cusco) and was for many years head of the Agronomy faculty. He catalogued many of Peru's thousands different sorts of potatoes and developed a few new varieties himself. (Comment from Gunilla Berglund August 2018)

## Back home at last

Mexico gave Hugo Blanco the chance to reassess his thinking, which as we have noted, moved in a more anarchist, indigenous and ecological way. This partly reflects discussions and reassessments being made in parts of the wider left. For example, the Fourth International over a period of at least three decades has come to embrace an approach which is explicitly feminist, ecosocialist and respectful of the contributions of peasants and indigenous people. Hugo also met his second wife in Mexico, a politically active teacher Ana Sandoval. They have two sons Marco and Bruno.

In 1997, the easing of conflict allowed Hugo to return to Peru. He lived for a while back at Chaupimayo. While the community did not organise as a communal *ayllu*, he noted that tasks were often shared, embodying the principle of *ayni* where work is shared and reciprocated, 'to sort out the issue of drinking water, to work on the plots owned by the community, to fix the roads, or to … install the satellite dish!' (Blanco 2018a: 156). He moved to the city of Cusco, living in the offices of the FDCC (Regional Federation of the Campesinos of Cusco), so he could travel more easily to different peasant communities (Blanco 2018a: 18).

Mining became more of a focus along with other environmental concerns. On 2 March 2001 the CCP issued a decree signed by Hugo Blanco, along with Washington Mendoza and Wilder Sanchez, for a general strike in Tambo Grande, Piura, in protest at the Canadian company Manhattan Minerals. The proposed open cast gold mine would have removed the settlement of Tambo Grande and polluted local water. A prominent opponent of the mine was murdered in the same year. A local referendum voted against it and the plan, was, for the time being, defeated (Martínez-Alier 2001: 264). Corporations had over taken *gamonales* as the main threat to *campesinos*.

Health concerns were to dominate Hugo Blanco's life in the early years of the new century. Numerous beatings by the police and prison guards, including some to the head, caused long term damage. Hugo has often joked that he has to wear a hat for medical reasons to avoid accidental injury. During 2002 he was in severe danger, and an international fundraising appeal, supported amongst others by the Fourth International, was launched to help him. After a successful operation in Mexico and treatment in Cuba, his activism has continued. Hugo Blanco thanked the Fourth International, greeting their congress, stating:

> The influence of various comrades meant that I could be operated on in Mexico and that, benefiting from Cuban solidarity, I was able to have exhaustive examinations in that country. And the moral force that I gained from the manifestation of sympathy from comrades from different countries was no small thing. Thanks to this solidarity, I conquered my illness and I am in good health. Naturally, as the comrades remind me, I am no longer 20 years old but nearer 70 and I cannot count on my body as I could. I can no longer run in the Andes according to my custom.
>
> On this occasion, like others when solidarity has saved my life, the Fourth International has played a central role. (Blanco 2003).

Eduardo Galeano recounts how, waking from the successful operation on his brain, Hugo feared that the surgeons had not only saved him but transplanted his thoughts, panicking that his radicalism had been surgically removed. However 'with his skull patched up, he continued to be the same Hugo as always [...] that smart crazy man who decided to be an Indian, even though he was not, and turned out to be the most Indian of all.' (Galeano 2018: 7).

Prior to going into surgery, Hugo was cautious about his chances of survival. Writing an autobiographical account of his struggles in 2002, he observed:

Old as I am, I have lived through phases of collective struggle outside of the law. For this reason I considered it my obligation to pass on this experience to the campesinos of today (Blanco 2018a: 18).

A continuity in Hugo Blanco's thought is that while he reassessed and sometimes criticised his previous political choices, he remained a revolutionary. He is a continuous militant, happy to both proclaim and practice direct action.

# 8

# Indigenous Struggles 2002-

'I've always fought for social equality. But now there's a more important problem: the survival of my species.' Hugo Blanco (Hamilton 2017)

In the twenty-first century, Hugo witnessed the growth of a New Latin American left, with leaders like Chavez in Venezuela and Morales in Bolivia winning elections. Hugo was increasingly committed to ecological matters, opposing big mining projects, and concerned with climate change. In 2006 he launched *Lucha Indigena*, a newspaper covering indigenous struggles in Peru and beyond. Noting that oppression has a cultural element, he has promoted Quechua language and culture including the traditional use of coca leaves.

## Koka Mama

Coca leaves are chewed in the Andes, where they have a social and cultural role. Like other plants cultivated by the Quechua-speaking people, they are viewed as sacred. Coca leaves are a mild stimulant and they have great nutritional value; their place in indigenous culture is extremely important. Hugo Blanco defends the use of coca leaves, while challenging the drugs industry producing cocaine. Cocaine was unknown among the indigenous, but as a synthesised product is a dangerous drug. Peru is one of the world's most important centres for cocaine production. Efforts, funded by the US government in particular, to outlaw cocaine have fuelled crime and corruption. The war on drugs, Hugo has observed, justifies the US setting up military bases in Latin America and terrorising the population.

Hugo was told by *campesino* comrades that Peru's official anti-drugs agency were taking coca leaves away from the people, who wished to chew them in the traditional way, and also involved in the drugs trade:

I have denounced in the pages of *Lucha Indigena* and on the radio, that in La Convención [the coca-growing zone of Cusco] they are manufacturing cocaine and the producers are the police chiefs of the zone and directors of ENACO (National Coca Company). I said that if that was slander, that they prosecute me for that reason. And nobody said anything.

I have gone to coca-growing zones like Valle del Río Apurímac y del Ene or Putina Punko (Sandia - Puno) and nobody has bothered me, but in (San Luis) La Convención when one travels by public transport and takes a few coca leaves to chew, they take it from you. (Blanco 2008b)

Hugo recognises the defence of the leaf as an essential part of the indigenous struggle. The preservation of indigenous culture is vital to indigenous dignity and the duplicity of US intervention demands exposure.

## Arrested again

The authorities did not persecute Hugo for calling out their complicity with the cocaine trade. However, he was arrested and imprisoned in Cusco in 2008:

The background is an illegal occupation of land belonging to the indigenous community of Huanoquite – Paruro (near Cusco, Peru), by the son of an ex-landowner. 50 years ago the landowner Paz was famous for branding his farmers with the same burning stick that he used to brand his animals. Hugo Blanco led the land struggle that resulted in the farmers themselves gaining ownership of the land. It is this same land that Paz's son is now illegally occupying. The police have taken the side of the landowner against the community, and have accused the farmers and Hugo Blanco of 'Resistance to authority'. They could not accuse the farmers of land occupation, since they actually hold the deeds for the land. In this accusation, they included Mr Blanco for having supported the community on previous occasions, despite the fact that he was not even there on the day the farmers decided to take back the land that is legally theirs. (Berglund 2008)

The court in Paruro had Hugo arrested on 2 October for failing to submit himself to the accusation of 'Resistance to authority'. However the court had failed to notify Hugo of the charge, which explained why he had not responded. Hugo was soon released without charge after the international campaign launched by his family. At the age of 73, this was the last time Hugo was imprisoned; happily this did not involve a hunger strike or beatings, nor did it end in exile.

## The pink tide

While it didn't quite sweep into Peru, much of Central and Latin America saw a pink tide of new left-wing governments, often sympathetic to indigenous people, win elections across the region in the early years of the twenty-first century. Hugo's attitude was, perhaps inevitably, contradictory. He recognised that the victories of left-wing leaders potentially opened up greater space for indigenous people, workers, and grassroots social movements to make positive change. However, he noted that these governments continued with mining and forms of economic development that harmed indigenous people and the environment. By 2010, Venezuela, Brazil, Paraguay, Ecuador and Argentina had all elected leaders on the left.

Hugo Chávez was elected Venezuelan President in 1998 and served until his death from cancer in 2013. After a coup attempt in 2002, he moved sharply to the left. He survived the coup because of support both from Cuba and strong grassroots mobilisation. Hugo Blanco argued that Chávez had learnt the lesson of Chile, that mobilising the population could prevent successful intervention by the USA (Ciccariello-Maher 2013: 177). In 2018 Venezuela is in crisis. Opponents argue that this shows that socialism is dysfunctional. The Venezuelan government point to US disruption of their economy, similar to the attempts to create food shortages and inflation in Chile that helped bring down Allende. Hugo has been critical, though, of many aspects of the governance of both Chávez and his successor Maduro, noting a tendency to centralise state control of social movements and a failure to consistently defend indigenous people. He condemned the right-wing opposition, in 2017, observing that the 'right are killing many Venezuelans, I hope that at some point the violence can stop and the people can govern.' (Zevallos 2017).

In January 2006, Hugo Blanco attended the inauguration of President Evo Morales in Bolivia. Bolivia had seen huge mobilisations by indigenous people and had a history of militant Trotskyism, represented by the indigenous working class in the form of the tin miners (John 2009). Morales, an Aymara speaking *campesino* and coca grower, sought to create a plurinational state, recognising the sovereignty of different indigenous nations. Hugo was enthusiastic about this political process, describing Morales' inauguration:

I was in Bolivia when the presidential mandate was transferred to Evo Morales. I was invited by comrade Evo. An atmosphere of revolutionary process floated in the air and imbued the people. It could be seen by the numbers who assembled and by the revolutionary fervour of people on the occasion of the big rallies.

You felt it on the occasion of the fighting speeches of Evo, who referred to Che and to the expression of Sub-commandant Marcos: 'command by obeying'. Evo spoke clearly against neo-liberalism. This atmosphere is also reflected in the fact that the Ministry of Justice is headed by a woman domestic servant who suffered physical, psychological and sexual abuse (Blanco 2008a: 12).

While progress was made in Bolivia, Hugo became aware as the years passed of weaknesses and betrayals. Morales has come into conflict with some indigenous groups in Bolivia:

The indigenous peoples have had a long struggle against Morales, who tried to open a highway through Tipnis, trampling indigenous populations and natural reserves. The government used police aggression in repressing the protests. Other popular sectors supported their struggle, until the government had to retreat. They have put forward a mining law which favors corporations without consulting the mostly indigenous farmers. (Saul 2015)

Ecuador elected a left government, supported by many indigenous people, but conflict with the indigenous has becoming increasingly common:

In the Ecuadorian constitution the rights of Mother Earth are considered, but in practice they promote their depredation. Correa is trying to impose mining in Cabecera de Cuenca, like the Conga project in Quimsacocha (*Tres Lagunas*). The indigenous people took me to the lakes, where we made offerings. Ecuador is also trying to exploit the oil in the natural reserve and indigenous territory of Yasuni. (Blanco in Saul 2015)

The academic and author Jeffrey Webber, who has been critical of the pacification of social movements by Latin American left governments, also makes this assessment:

These center-left governments achieved myriad social gains. Alternative regional integration projects began to develop in opposition to American dominance. The Argentine Supreme Court declared laws that granted immunity to leading figures of the dictatorship unconstitutional, and constituent assemblies in Venezuela, Bolivia, and Ecuador inserted some transformative elements into their countries' new constitutions. Politically, the contrast with the repressive governments in Colombia, Peru, Paraguay,

Honduras, and Mexico is stark. Ideologically, anti-imperialist discourse was revived, and, in some places, strategic debates over socialism and paths of transition to post-capitalism proliferated (Webber 2017a).

Such states have promoted social equality and respect for indigenous people and have made some economic progress. Yet faced with reliance on capitalist economic relations they have not been able to move to fully ecological economies. The US has also continued to destabilise them. In Peru, although Ollanta Humala was elected in 2011, on a platform that showed some sympathies with the pink tide governments, he continued many of the environmentally damaging policies of previous presidents like Alan Garcia:

> The situation in Peru is perfectly plain. Ollanta Humala sides openly with developmentalism. Ever since his electoral campaign, he has promised to promote open-pit mining and agroindustry, each a force for environmental degradation. (Blanco 2011b: 2)

In the 2016 Presidential election, the left candidate, Verónica Mendoza of the Broad Front, gained 19 per cent of the vote, coming third. She had Hugo's cautious support (Blanco 2015b).

## Lucha Indigena

Since 2006 Hugo Blanco has published the monthly newspaper *Lucha Indigena* (Indigenous Struggle). It promotes an indigenous perspective and, while written in Spanish, contains some material in Quechua. It has an internationalist outlook, covering not only struggles in Peru and the wider Americas but globally. It contains news items about strikes and protests in the USA, Britain and even Greece. Issue number 143, from July 2018, which is typical, contains an editorial condemning US President Trump, not as a single crazy individual, but as a representative of a capitalist system destroying the environment. Hugo noted that Trump imprisoned refugees forced to move by the extreme weather patterns caused by climate change. Hugo makes use of the internet to keep in touch with comrades and events across the planet.

Around the start of the twenty-first century, the CCP and other movements defined themselves increasingly around an indigenous rather than a peasant identity. While, Morales's victory encouraged Hugo to set up *Lucha Indigena,* he later noted, '"Brother Evo" is looking more like a distant cousin lately' (Blanco 2011b: 2). *Lucha Indigena* criticises developmentalist policies that promote roads and other big capital projects which damage the environment and indigenous communities.

One of the most important and dramatic struggles covered by *Lucha Indigena* occurred in 2009, when the indigenous peoples of the Peruvian Amazon rose up to oppose gas and oil exploitation of the forests. Alan Garcia, once again President of Peru representing APRA, continued to move right. He was committed to neoliberal policies including accelerating mining and other forms of extraction in the country. As elsewhere in Latin America, the state claimed ownership of land below the surface, thus Garcia sold the rights to prospect for gas and oil to various foreign corporations as part of a free trade agreement with the USA (Blanco 2018a: 96).

Fearing the damage that this would do to local communities and the Amazon, AIDESEP, Inter-ethnic Association for the Development of the Peruvian Rainforest, a coalition of different indigenous Amazon groups, acted. They blocked roads and river traffic protesting at this planned destruction of the Amazon. This increasingly militant struggle led to the Bagua massacre, on 5 June, on World Environment Day. As thousands of Awajún and Wampis people blocked the road at the 'Devil's Bend' as part of the ongoing protest, the security services opened fire. The conflict led to the deaths of both indigenous protestors and police officers. While the authorities claimed that only ten indigenous people had been killed by their forces, AIDESEP argued that figure was closer two hundred and that many people had been wounded (Blanco 2018a: 100).

*Lucha Indigena* was used to raise both Peruvian and international solidarity for the indigenous. Both Hugo and AIDESEP viewed the struggle as one to protect the international environment, arguing that the Amazon is the lungs of the planet and that increased extraction of gas and oil would lead to greater climate change:

> The Amazonian natives knew that what is at stake is their own survival. We hope that the world population becomes aware that they are fighting in defence of all humankind, the Amazon jungle is the lungs of the planet (Blanco 2018a: 99)

Demonstrations were held in solidarity in Lima, Cusco and other Peruvian cities. International action saw protests at Peruvian Embassies around the world. Later, the law opening up the Amazon was reversed. The struggles have continued; in 2016 the indigenous protection NGO Survival International reported that the indigenous on trial for killing police officers had been acquitted, but noted that 70 per cent of the Peruvian Amazon was now available to oil companies to exploit. The militancy of AIDESEP has also continued with Amazonian nations gaining solidarity from other indigenous people across the planet.

## 2010 European tour

Hugo Blanco's increasing stature as an advocate of ecosocialism brought him back to Europe in 2010. A British tour was organised in the autumn of 2010 by two ecosocialist groups. Socialist Resistance is a British organisation which collaborates with Trotsky's Fourth International, while Green Left is an anti-capitalist network within the Green Party of England and Wales. Hugo spoke to audiences in London, Bristol, Cardiff, Birmingham and other centres, as well as travelling to meetings in Scotland, Ireland and other parts of Europe. He was hosted by the Scottish Socialist Party in Scotland. He took part in a fringe meeting at the Green Party conference held in Birmingham on 11 September 2010. He was critical of what he described as 'biblical Marxism' that treated Marx's writing as if they were 'holy scripture'.

Adam Johannes who organised a meeting in Cardiff, described the experience:

In October 2010 on a cold dark Welsh night, 150 people crowded into a packed hall in Cardiff to hear Hugo Blanco speak. The audience was diverse, young students and environmentalists, Plaid Cymru supporters, anarchists, long time radicals and old school socialists asking questions about the role of the rural peasantry and urban working class in the revolution.

Joining Hugo on the platform was Eli Valencia from the leadership of the Chilean group – *Movimiento de los Pueblos y los Trabajadores* (People and Workers' Movement – MPT). Eli spoke passionately of her people's dream of a peaceful road to socialism crushed when she was at school by Pinochet's coup and her role in the underground struggle against the dictatorship, she closed by talking about the opportunities in Chile and the continent as a whole.

The audience left enthused by Hugo Blanco's vision of a new socialism and an ecology of the global south that centred people and planet. While we were offered something new, much of the discussion from the floor also looked back to the long struggle of the Latin American masses with words uttered like Paulo Freire, Evo Morales, Hugo Chavez, Liberation Theology, Che Guevara, Salvador Allende.

The meeting was chaired by Marianne Owens now on the national executive of the PCS union. Having heard her mention at the meeting that there would be a PCS march against the announcement of the closure of the Newport Passport Office by the Con-Dem government in a few days, the day after the meeting she and workers were thrilled to receive the following short message from Hugo:

'I want to express my solidarity with those struggling against cuts and redundancies in public services like the Passport Office in Newport. The government dominated by big multinational businesses is unloading the crisis which they have caused onto the shoulders of working people. These are the same companies that are killing indigenous peoples by destroying our mother nature. In solidarity, Hugo Blanco, *Lucha Indigena* (Indigenous Struggle), Peru'

Hugo spoke at the launch of *The Rise of the Green Left* book, along with Jeremy Corbyn MP, who was then a back-bench member of parliament but later became Labour Party leader. Everywhere Hugo spoke, he reminded audiences that we needed to put an end to capitalism before it puts an end to us.

## Mining and other recent struggles

In the last decade, huge protests against mines have occurred, particularly in the North of Peru. At least 20 per cent of the country has been granted to various projects to extract minerals, oil or gas (Saul 2015). This has sparked huge resistance from social movements and indigenous people and led to over a hundred and fifty conflicts related to mining. The Conga project, an open-cast gold mine in the north of the country, was abandoned after huge opposition in 2016. *Lucha Indigena* carries stories of the resistance to such projects each month.

The Hugo Blanco Galdos School for Environmental and Social Leaders was established in August 2016, by Plataforma Interinstitucional de Celendín (PIC), a network of more than thirty groups opposing mining. Hugo attended the launch of his school for activists. Milton Sanchez, PIC's coordinator described it as

a space for mutual learning through the sharing of ideas and experiences to define the necessary steps to defend the environment from irreparable damage, while proposing practical alternatives to the notion that extractivism – the exploitation and plunder of natural resources at any cost, is the only way. (Anon 2016)

An attempt in 2017 to pardon the former president Fujimori was possible because of power struggles between the elected Peruvian President Pedro Pablo Kuczynski and Fujimori's followers. Kuczynski had been elected during a second round of votes with transfers from those who opposed the election of a rival candidate, Fujimori's daughter Keiko. Without a majority, the President avoided impeachment by promising to pardon Fujimori. The latter had been convicted in 2007 for crimes including accepting bribes, paying $15 million from state funds to his intelligence service chief Vladimiro Montesinos, and committing human rights abuses. Hugo, having just turned 83, campaigned against Fujimori's release.

Asked about his most recent struggles, in 2017, Hugo focused upon environmental issues:

> My fight now is for water, I am also with the Amazonians who fight in defence of the rainforest, which are the lungs of the world. I am also against agro-industry, because it practices monoculture that is impoverishing the earth, because they put chemical fertilizers on the land. They also use insecticides and herbicides that are killing nature, they do not worry about killing the land because after killing the land cultivated here, the multinationals can go to Asia and Africa, to continue killing the land. They also produce for export, growing artichokes and asparagus that suck up a lot of water, taking away the water that should be for Peruvians. (Zevallos 2017).

## Hugo Blanco on ecosocialism and resistance

While the twenty-first century has been gentler for Hugo, with to date only one arrest, and no exiles, the militancy he has engaged in since he was a boy has continued. This shows a continuity in action and ideas, but in the twenty-first century he has increasingly linked social struggles to indigenous rights and indigenous rights to global campaigning against capitalism and for an ecosocialist alternative.

It is possible from reading Hugo's numerous editorials, interviews and speeches from the second decade of the twenty-first century to outline his linked analysis of ecosocialism, social movement protest and indigenous struggles. Climate change is perhaps the most important manifestation of a tendency to make our planet less and less habitable for human beings and other species. Environmental destruction is driven, Hugo often argues, by the demands of corporations to make profit. Oil exploration may threaten the future, but short-term financial gain is put before long term sustainability. Profit functions within a global capitalist system and is still, despite the growth of cyber space and renewable energy, extractivist. The drive to take minerals and metals from the ground is environmentally destructive, but is necessary within this economic system:

> Most current struggles of indigenous campesinos are against the killing of Pachamama, Mother Earth; against depredations by the large companies, mainly mining, but also petroleum and gas. Previous Peruvian governments were servants of feudal lords; today they serve the great multinationals. They act against the Peruvian people and against nature. (Blanco 2008a: 10).

Hugo is well aware that Latin American economies are locked into the capitalist system, and even when they apparently promote indigenous and ecological values have tended to base their economies on extraction. Thus, Venezuela extracts oil, Bolivia is still largely dependent on gas and Ecuador exports both commodities. Peru has a large mining sector. It is thus not just a matter of ending capitalism, an alternative economy must also respect nature. The economic models that we are familiar with are shaped by patterns of imperialism. European peoples have invaded other parts of the world, enslaving and exterminating existing populations, and devastating the environment.

Hugo argues that while indigenous people might not use the term 'ecosocialist', they have been fighting for ecosocialism for five hundred years (Weinberg 2009). The indigenous in the Andes and the Amazon believe:

> humanity is a daughter of and part of Mother Earth. We must live in her bosom in harmony with her. Each hill or peak, each river, each vegetable or animal species has a spirit. (Blanco 2008a: 7)

Until Latin American states move beyond extractivist economies, they will be dependent on global capitalism and will continue to contribute to environmental destruction. Moving to an ecological economy will not be easy, but indigenous people provide useful lessons for attempting to do so. Indigenous notions of ecological collective ownership via commons such as the *ayllu* are part of this. Indigenous and other forms of resistance to ecological destructive projects are part of the ecosocialist struggle. Indigenous economies based on concepts of 'enough' rather than constant profit and growth provide an alternative to extractivism.

Marxist analysis of capitalism has much value in seeking to understand and challenge ecological destruction. While some Marxists have been equally as hostile to environmental protection as capitalists, there are strong ecological comments in the works of Marx and Engels (Thornett forthcoming). Marx and Engels were also fascinated by indigenous societies (Rosemont 2009).

Despite the criticism of those like Peruvian novelist Mario Vargas Llosa of 'indigenists', Hugo Blanco and allied thinkers are not primitivists who reject modern society or romantics looking back to a past imagined golden age:

> We are defending our culture in its diverse aspects: our cosmic vision, social organization, our rituals and agricultural know-how, medicine, music, language, and many others.
> We do not claim that our culture is superior to others. We are struggling to stop it from being considered inferior.
> We want to be respected as equals.
> We have been educated to harmonize equality and diversity. Peru is a mega-diverse country, both geographically and demographically. We have 82 per cent of the world's 103 natural life zones. Our inhabitants speak 45 different languages. The great Inca Sun God celebration was not exclusive. It had a procession of different peoples with diverse gods. The notion of 'one God' did not exist. We are for the equality of the diverse; we are against homogenization (igualitarismo).
> On the one hand we respect diverse individualities and particularities. On the other, we oppose individualism. Ours is a culture of solidarity.
> We don't seek a return to the past. We know we must make the best in general of advances in human culture.
> That does not contradict our resolve to go back to our own roots. Our past will be vividly present in our future.
> We love and care for Pachamama. We fervently yearn to return to basing our economy on our rich biodiversity, through agriculture and natural medicine, along with any modern advances that do no harm. (Blanco 2008a: 11).

*Lucha Indigena* is written by and for indigenous people but contains news of trade union and other working-class struggles.

Hugo Blanco, as noted, now promotes a Zapatista rather than a Leninist approach to revolution. Asked in 2009 if he was still a Trotskyist, he argued that the conflict between Trotsky and Stalin occurred within a particular historical context and is less relevant in the twenty-first century:

I defended Trotsky because the struggle was against Stalinism. Am I still a Trotskyist? I'm not sure. In certain senses I am, and in others I am not. Trotsky believed in defending the revolutionary ideas of Marx and Lenin against bureaucratic tendencies. He defended world revolution against the ideas of 'socialism in one country' and a 'progressive bourgeoisie' and 'revolution by stages' and the other Stalinist ideas promoted in the name of Marxism-Leninism. So I was right to be a Trotskyist in this epoch. [...]

But now that there is no Stalinism, why do I have to be a Trotskyist? I don't feel the same imperative. Of course, there are things I have learned from Marx, things I have learned from Lenin, things I have learned from Trotsky – and from other revolutionaries, from Rosa Luxemburg, from Antonio Gramsci, from Che Guevara. But now I do not feel it is logical to form a Trotskyist party. [...] We don't have to resuscitate old debates from the last century. It is enough to still believe that another world is possible. I am old, and if I can teach something about Marx, Lenin and Trotsky and so on, this is something I can contribute. I still believe in standing up and struggling and not pleading with the government, so in this sense I am still a Trotskyist. But I don't feel the need to say, 'Listen everybody, this Trotskyism is the answer!' (Weinberg 2009)

## Deep green Marxism

Hugo Blanco believes that the ecological crisis is an immediate threat to humanity and the focus of struggles must be to end the capitalist system that generates this threat. While Hugo largely rejects labels, his work might inform the development of what the theologian and philosopher Ted Stolze (2017) has called 'deep green Marxism'.

Deep ecology was coined by the philosopher Arne Næss. He challenged human exceptionalism, noting that human beings are one species amongst many and we humans should respect other forms of life. This has been contrasted with an apparent 'shallow ecology', that values environmental protection primarily because it benefits we humans. Climate change threatens the human species, so from a shallow ecology point of view we should work to reduce the burning of fossil fuels which will make life more and more difficult for us.

From a deep ecology point of view, not only do we have to save the humans, but we also should care for the rest of nature. Næss based his deep ecology on the teachings of the Dutch-Jewish seventeenth century philosopher Spinoza. Spinoza argued that there is no kingdom within nature. By this he meant that, rather than human beings having their own dominion, we are ultimately part of nature and governed by its rules (Montag 1998:x).

Næss called for an 'ecological egalitarianism' and argued that different species were nodes within a wider field. He suggested that deep ecologists should favour diversity:

> of human ways of life, of cultures, of occupations, of economies. They support the fight against economic and cultural, as much as military, invasion and domination, and they are opposed to the annihilation of seals and whales as much as to that of human tribes or cultures. (Næss 1973: 96)

While Næss's intention to construct a radical philosophy of ecological politics was laudable, deep ecology, in practice, has often been problematic. Nature encompasses everything, not just humans and parrots or even apes and microbes, but stars, as well as every product of human labour, from fridges to operas. If all of nature is valued, how do we distinguish between one part or another, how do we find criteria for any particular action? We can argue that anything that promotes life and the diversity of life should be valued but there has been a second, serious problem with deep ecology. It has tended to be interpreted in a right-wing way, arguing that human beings are a product of nature and seeing nature in a Social Darwinist form. Shockingly in the 1980s the deep ecology direct action network Earth First! activists David Foreman and Chris Manes, argued that both AIDS and the Ethiopian famine were beneficial because they reduced human numbers and thus protected the environment (Shantz 2012: 60). Earth First! in recent decades rejected these right-wing articulations but deep ecology remains tainted; the social ecologist Murry Bookchin engaged in vigorous and justified criticism (Bookchin 1993).

In recent decades, Marxism has been seen as one basis for a form of social ecology. A growing ecosocialist literature has drawn upon the ecological writings of Marx and Engels, who, despite the common disregard of many twentieth century Marxists for the environment, were concerned with problems such as deforestation and soil erosion (Thornett forthcoming). Marxism might be seen as both sophisticated in exploring the social causes of ecological crisis, a discussion which is referred to by Hugo Blanco, while at the same time a rather human centred discourse. Now as humans we are inevitably humanist, putting ourselves at the centre of things, but ecology and ecological politics, perhaps require that we acknowledge the more modest view that we are just part of life, not its apex or core. Ted Stolze's suggestion, briefly outlined in a book review, is that a deep green Marxism would include respect for other species (Stolze 2017).

Hugo notes 'I'm a Quechua indigenous person, and we have a principle of love and the worship of nature, which in Quechua we call Pachamama, or Mother Nature'. (Hamilton 2017). Styling himself a son of Pachamama, he has noted that the indigenous Quechua commons, the *ayllu,* includes in its communities plants, animals, rivers and forests. Mountains, such as Ausangate in Cusco's Vilcanota, are beings, the Apus. The 'indigenous talk with them, they are their protectors'. (Interview 2018). He argued 'across the whole continent our indigenous culture is respectful of Mother Earth, for example *Mapuche* means Child of the Earth'. (Blanco 2008b).

Leon Trotsky maintained that human action would reshape nature and had little time for discussions with Apus or the celebration of plants:

> Through the machine, man in Socialist society will command nature in its entirety, with its grouse and its sturgeons. He will point out places for mountains and for passes. He will change the course of the rivers, and he will lay down rules for the oceans. (Trotsky 1955: 252)

Given that such sentiments were common when he wrote and that no thinker is the prophet of all virtue, condemnation of Trotsky on ecological grounds may appear misplaced. He did also note that nature is both literally universal and subject to change and transformation, with or without the human element. Even human tools are part of nature:

> this dualism of earth and machine is false; one can contrast a backward peasant field with a flour mill, either on a plantation, or in a Socialist society. The poetry of the earth is not eternal, but changeable, and man began to sing articulate songs only after he had placed between himself and the earth implements and instruments which were the first simple machines. (Trotsky 1955: 252)

Nonetheless, a little more respect for non–human nature might be eco-logically and ethically appropriate. Yet, in the same way that respect for the indigenous and concern for ecology are being read in Marx and Engels work, perhaps there is also a largely unread Trotsky who might have had more time for Hugo's indigeneity and respect for the rest of nature.

S. Sándor John's book *Bolivia's Radical Traditions*, subtitled *Permanent Revolution in the Andes*, notes that during the late 1930s in Mexico, Trotsky became interested in the revolutionary potential of the peoples of the Andes. A Bolivian diplomat Alfredo Sanjines met him, and they discussed the concept of the *ayllu*. Trotsky agreed with Sanjines that the *ayllu* might provide the basis for a collectivist socialist form of agriculture.

The *ayllu* is rather more than a simple commons or collective, but it's interesting that Trotsky was introduced to it as a concept. Sadly, with his murder in 1940, he was unable to develop a study of a distinctively Andean approach to Marxism. Sándor John has, however, shown how the Bolivian Trotskyist movement embraced indigenous concepts, based as it was on Quechua and Aymara speakers. One of the illustrations in his book shows a photograph of Trotskyist militants Carlos Salazar and Ana Pérez sat in front of an image of the earth mother goddess *Pachamama* holding a hammer and sickle (John 2009: 67). The continuities and breaks between Trotskyism and the indigenous revolutions in the Andes are fascinating.

In 1928 Luis Eduardo Valcárcel (1891-1987), a Peruvian anthropologist, prophesised the coming of the 'Indian Lenin' who would bring dignity 'to the Indian, that Lord of the land, creation of the Andes, granite symbol of an immortal culture'. (Starn 1999: 228). While he would reject Valcárcel's description and Hugo Blanco is no longer a Leninist, like Lenin Hugo is concerned with understanding how to make revolutionary change. The richness of his experience may inform how we struggle for a diverse, just and ecological future. This is the subject of chapter nine which concludes this book.

# 9

# Change the system not the climate

Of course I am an ecosocialist, as are the indigenous peoples, even though they don't use the term. I believe along with indigenous peoples that it is the collective which rules, not the individual. The indigenous peoples and I defend Mother Nature, water, and forests, so we are ecologists. Hugo Blanco (Saul 2015)

Climate change is an increasingly obvious threat. During the summer of 2018 extreme weather events occurred across the planet. In Tokyo, the heatwave killed many people. In Greece and Sweden forest fires raged. In California, apocalyptic images showed vast areas consumed by flames. As I write, huge floods are devastating southern India and have killed hundreds; 'Kerala's chief minister, Pinarayi Vijayan, says the flooding is the worst the state has seen in 100 years' (Anon 2018). Climate change will accelerate such disasters and cause other appalling consequences such as ocean acidification. The Canadian writer and activist Naomi Klein argues that

we need a new form of democratic eco-socialism, with the humility to learn from Indigenous teachings about the duties to future generations and the interconnection of all of life, appears to be humanity's best shot at collective survival. (Klein 2018).

Indigenous teachings on ecology are vital. A variety of authors, for example, de Castro (2015), argue that indigenous perspectives can enrich social and political theory. Equally Hugo's sustained thoughtful militancy is a good basis for enhancing ecosocialist strategies for transcending capitalism.

Hugo Blanco's work in recent decades has been to help support militant resistance to damaging projects that threaten both local environments and planetary ecology. *Lucha Indigena* is a diary of struggles, across the Americas and beyond, against extractivism, using direct action. This resistance is undertaken primarily but not exclusively by indigenous people. Bagua in the Amazon is one example; the resistance to mining projects in the North of Peru is another. In Canada, the Idle No More movement formed by First Nations women challenged the polluting Tar Sands project. Environmental movements, ecosocialists and Green parties should prioritise such kinds of resistance; in Britain, for example, there are vigorous movements against fracking.

Hugo Blanco's revolutionary life, whether campaigning for land rights or protecting the environment, has been about robust action; the politics of pressure to resist the powerful. He has maintained practical solidarity with grassroots social movements. We should, like him, make our ecological commitments practical, precise and militant.

## System change

Power can be conceived as occurring within a particular system; to change the system it must be understood. Trotsky argued,

> In politics as in private life there is nothing cheaper than moralizing – nothing cheaper or more useless. Many people, however, find it attractive because it saves them from having to look into the objective mechanism of events. (Trotsky 1980: 90)

The 'mechanism of events' reveals that a society is neither purely the product of chance nor based on subjective choice of any particular group, however powerful. A society, to some extent, is a system with a particular dynamic. Where the mass media acknowledges environmental problems, the response they are most likely to suggest is individual. Environmental solutions are presented most commonly by the media in terms of personal change and lobbying. Climate change may encourage us to consume less, recycling may be seen as beneficial and it is assumed perhaps that governments can introduce laws that will promote renewable energy or outlaw plastic bags, but Hugo Blanco's emphasis is different. While it is important to live in a more environmentally friendly way, and for governments to make legislative changes, environmental problems also demand militant action. Climate change is a product of the system we live within: capitalism. Hugo argues that we have to change the system:

> Capitalism's sacred principle is to earn the greatest possible amount of money in the shortest possible time. It doesn't matter whether pursuing this principle brings about the death of humanity, including the capitalists' own grandchildren.

We are not speaking of a group of evil people who consciously want to do away with the human race but the maelstrom of the capitalist system, itself. If one or another capitalist were to set up a factory that did not pollute, at a cost to his profits, the business would be uncompetitive and would likely be replaced by another that was not so scrupulous. We cannot have capitalism without global warming. Warming is inherent in the capitalist system and cannot be stopped so as long as we live in a world ruled by capital. On the contrary, it will get steadily worse, until our species is exterminated. (Blanco 2010b)

Deep seated systemic change is necessary. This provides an apparent contradiction. When we work for change, our demands may, even if achieved, do nothing to transform the system, but if we reject reforms we can end up doing nothing. One alternative is the purity of inaction the other is action that reforms a system so as to conserve it. All avenues can, for the ecological left, appear blocked. Hugo Blanco's approach has been to contrast capitalism with an alternative system, the *ayllu*. The *ayllu* has many positive features and some negative ones, but it functions with a different logic. Creating alternatives to capitalism is necessary, and the *ayllu* might provide a seed to do this.

## Concepts and contexts

Marx, Trotsky and Lenin, and other Marxists, built a conceptual apparatus for understanding how capitalism works and how it can be systematically transformed. The need for intense struggle and systematic change demand both militancy and clear concepts to guide action. Marxist-Leninist groups, including the Shining Path as an extreme example, embraced Mao's dictum that the 'correctness or incorrectness of the ideological and political line decides everything' (Mao quoted in Elbaum 2018: 157). The line is based on supposedly proven concepts. The pursuit of conceptual clarity can, however, lead to fanaticism, violence and delusion. Many Marxist political parties, groups, and internationals have used conceptual difference to maintain separate sectarian identities. Concepts can rather than being used as tools for understanding social change become methods of maintaining particular sectarian identities.

Hugo Blanco has written that we must remember that 'every word Marx or Trotsky wrote was contextually specific'. (Ward 2011: 662). Attempting to understand the 'objective mechanism of events' is necessary, but a certain modesty is needed too; we may misunderstand the mechanism, misapply the elements of the mechanism or fail to understand how it works in a particular context.

Mariátegui observed, in this regard, the interplay between concepts and context in Marxism:

> Marxism, of which all speak but few know or above all comprehend, is a fundamentally dialectic method. It is a method that is completely based in reality, on facts. It is not, as some erroneously suppose, a body of principles of rigid consequences, the same of all historical climates and all social latitudes. Marx extracted his method from history's guts. Marxism, in every country, in every people, operates and acts on the environment, on the medium, without neglecting any of its modalities. (Mariátegui in Webber 2017b: 119)

Hugo Blanco has emphasised the importance of listening to others, noting that one must 'listen to the people and participate in their struggles.' (Huilca 2012). Understanding what to do in a particular situation, if you like 'the correct line', cannot be developed  without paying close attention to context and listening to peasants, workers and other communities in struggle. Resistance requires practical understanding: Hugo's practical approach has much value, he noted that when he went to Chaupimayo:

> The *compañeros* wanted me to be always in front of the typewriter, but I liked agricultural work; I also understood that this had a political importance, because in the informal conversations between work breaks, we would talk about the problems of the struggle, so that when the assembly was held, these problems were easy to solve. Difference in workers assemblies are very important, in the workers' assemblies, due to lack of time, sometimes differences are voted upon without having dissected the problems. (Interview July 2018)

## Culture and language

Hugo's approach to social change is based on resistance: resistance that is informed by strong concepts (capitalism, collectivism, colonialism, ecology, etc) and is sensitive to context. Culture, based on signs and practices, is also seen as a vital element of resistance. He is known for his keen interest in indigenous culture. Cultural politics that builds identities glues communities of resistance together, and through such culture, alternative ways of being can be sustained.

Language is an essential element of culture is. The use of *foci*-based guerrilla strategies may have failed in Peru in the mid-1960s, partly because the guerrillas generally spoke Spanish rather than the Quechua of the *campesinos*.

The politics of language is important, the use of English or Spanish or other colonial languages act as tools of domination. Frederic Jameson, in books such as *The Prison-House of Language*, notes that language helps structure our social reality (Jameson 1975). While outright violence is a form of control, so is control of language.

Hugo has, from his childhood into his eighties, stressed the practical and ideological importance of speaking Quechua, the language of the indigenous people of the Andes, and shown how its displacement has been used to oppress. Reclaiming language is part of the politics of liberation and social transformation.

Rather than reducing power to economics, Marxism, at its most sophisticated, examines how both the domination of elites and the transformative resistance of workers, is based on a complex interaction of politics, economics and culture (Thompson 1975). Language struggles are struggles for socialism and for a diverse, democratic future. The dignity of human beings means that diverse languages and literatures should be defended, but defence of language can also be linked to questions of human survival. Indigenous languages may provide concepts to create more ecological and equal structures. Silences too can be important. The concept of 'good living' expresses the idea of living in an environmentally friendly way and has been expressed in Spanish as *'buen vivir'* and posed as an alternative to extractivist economics. In turn, in Quechua, such good living can be read as *'Sumak Kawsay'*. However Hugo once told me that this was not a concept expressed in such words traditionally because it was so obvious that good living was important, that such a common sense was not spoken. Who would debate whether 'good living' was better than 'bad living'?

A system makes some things possible and others unthinkable. Language is part of this. European colonialists were keen to destroy the languages they found, so that the indigenous cultures they invaded would be weakened or erased. This was legitimised with notions of progress, linked even with Darwinism, suggesting that successful languages grow in the number of speakers and the depth of their communication. From a Eurocentric perspective, it is argued that 'inferior' languages are spoken by fewer and fewer people, and gradually disappear. Languages, in fact don't so much die of natural causes, but are murdered by the weapons of the invader.

In Peru, the conflict between two views of language is expressed in the work of the two novelists, Arguedas and Vargas Llosa. Arguedas valued linguistic diversity, writing in both Spanish and Quechua, celebrating culture from the Andes. In contrast, Llosa wrote in Spanish, rejecting Quechua as an appropriate language for the novel, short story or comment piece. He views the problems of Peru as a product of an archaic past, and has little interest in indigenous cultures. The conflict of novelists is the conflict of meaning, and meaning shapes our realities. And as argued earlier, Vargas Llosa attacked the work of Arguedas within this framework, whereas Hugo defended it as being an expression of the struggle to defend and develop an indigenous way of being in today's context (Blanco 2018a).

Hugo consistently promotes and defends the Quechua language, in a way which recalls the Nigerian playwright and poet Wole Soyinka's argument for cultural retrieval in opposition to colonialism as the 'conscious activity of recovering what has been hidden, lost, repressed, denigrated, or indeed simply denied' (Soyinka 1990: 114).

The anthropologist Marisol De La Cadena, who incidentally has worked with Hugo in a wonderful study of indigenous seers from Cusco who communicate with the earth beings, particularly mountains, references Bruno Latour's idea of a 'stronghold'. This is a language into which the concepts of others are transferred and thus distorted:

> Whatever people do and wherever they go, they have to pass through the contender's position and to help him/her further his/her own interests – it also has a linguistic sense, so that one version of the language game translates all the others, replacing them with 'whatever you wish. This is really what you mean' (Latour in De La Cadena 2015: 300)

Europeans have 'translated' the desires of the Quechua speakers into their own concepts, thus ignoring challenges that might be posed by different ways of understanding the world and relationships. A powerful part of politics is to pull down such strongholds and to listen. Listening provides access to new concepts and ways of being. This is a part of anti-colonial struggle, which challenges Eurocentrism and potentially provides for new forms of ecological living.

## Violence and non-violence

Hugo Blanco has, throughout his life, argued that the rich and powerful don't take challenges to their authority lightly. Positive social change may be met with force, so we must be prepared. Militarists argue that violence is the key tactic used to create change, Hugo rejects this; resistance and defence can take many forms. Revolutionary transformation may include moments of violence, but these are often slight. For example, the Bolshevik Revolution of 1917 was largely bloodless (Rai 2017).

Hugo Blanco, during the 1960s, was explicit in his support for the Cuban revolution, seeing it as a blow to imperialism and an affirmation of Trotsky's notion of permanent revolution, even though, of course, Che and Castro were not Trotskyists. However, while far from being a pacifist, he suggested that armed struggle was no substitute for the patient work of supporting workers and peasants in struggle, along with creating a viable Leninist Party, as steps towards revolution. In particularly, he felt that a *foci* approach might lead to the 'substitution of audacious actions by a courageous group for mass actions' (Blanco 1977: 75). The problem, he felt, was not even necessarily the actions of the Cuban revolutionaries but their interpretation of them by others on the left. While in the twenty-first century Hugo is not a Leninist, embracing instead the more decentralist approach of those like the Zapatistas, continuity in his thinking remains clear. Popular mobilisation, patiently sustained, is the path to resistance; guerrilla action by the few is inadequate.

Interviewed in 2010, Hugo observed that there was no master plan for an armed uprising in La Convención:

It was important that I knew that the struggle would become violent. Revolutionaries always know that things will be settled violently even before it is true in their own case, Marx teaches us that violence is part of history. But I couldn't say so. I couldn't say, 'this thing will only end in armed conflict and we have to prepare!' They would have thrown me out on my ear, because the truth is that people don't like violence. When their lives are at stake, people want things to be solved peacefully, by law. When they see that the law doesn't work, then they have to resort to other measures: strikes, occupations, marches, etc. But these measures only gain popularity when the legal routes have been exhausted. And ultimately, if and when the enemy attacks violently, and they have no other recourse, then the people too will see the need to defend themselves violently. (Ward 2010: 653)

Although violence was part of the uprising in La Convención, it was largely one sided. Overwhelming violence was meted out by the *gamonales*, happy to massacre *campesinos*. The strikes and land occupations that proved so successful were largely non-violent; the *campesinos'* use of arms was modest and defensive. One of Hugo Blanco's most important contributions to the understanding of social change is thus his nuanced approach to the question of conflict, cutting across the binary choices of violence and non-violence for social movements.

Hugo has been supportive of the struggles by the Kurdish people to build a self-governing, feminist and ecological society. While Syria is a long way from Peru, he has shown a keen interest in their work, noting that their creation of citizens' militias, often women-led, have allowed them to challenge the destructive forces of the so-called Islamic State:

> We have seen how the armed Kurdish militias – formed of both women and men, democratically organized by the oppressed – dealt the Islamic State its greatest defeat yet by throwing it out of Kobane. (Blanco 2015a)

Hugo, back in the 1970s, argued that guerrilla tactics, or indeed other tactics, might be mistaken for strategy, arguing that 'concrete reality' matters:

> I am against the guerrilla 'strategy' as I would be against the 'strategy' of the general strike, the 'strategy' of strikes with factory occupations, the barricades 'strategy'. These are all very useful tactics, which can be used in certain countries under certain circumstances, applying them to the concrete reality of each country at the given moment. (Blanco 1974: 991)

## Revolutionary biography

Hugo's life shows the various biographical stages and processes that those of us seeking social change may go through. Aware of oppression from an early age, he had to decide which side to take. While his family had a mixed background he sided with the oppressed. At university, he rejected his studies in agronomy because he knew that the future of this would likely involve working for powerful landowners. He was attracted to the militancy of the Trotskyists, a militancy that he has continued to take as his basic attitude.

Hugo's life has involved much personal sacrifice. It is necessary to acknowledge and prepare for this. The biography of any serious revolutionary can potentially involve arrest, beatings, imprisonment and exile. For those of us who advocate social change, solidarity is essential, supporting prisoners, promoting human rights and resisting deportation are all practices that we much prioritise. A small piece of personal action that goes further is writing to political prisoners and campaigning for their freedom. There are many forgotten green political prisoners; as I write, Red Fawn Fallis, from the Oglala Sioux tribe, is serving three years in prison, after being set up by an informant. She was arrested along with nearly eight hundred people, mainly indigenous, for opposing an oil pipeline at Standing Rock, North Dakota (Hand 2018). The militants defend the Earth and we must defend them too. Groups like Earth First! and Anarchist Black Cross publish lists of green and other political prisoners. It's important to remember that one of the most important features of Hugo's story has been the massive and effective international campaigns of solidarity when his life has been in danger.

On another occasion in the 1980s, Hugo's comrade Javier Diez Canseco from the PUM (*Partido Unificado Mariateguista*), fearing that Hugo was to be 'disappeared' by the forces of President Alan Garcia, sat in front of the wheel of a plane that was trying to take off with Hugo on board (Blanco 2018a: 91). Moments before, he had physically sat on Hugo to try to prevent him being dragged off. Hugo was saved, the plane didn't take off. While it is rare to see such drama, defence of revolutionaries and resisters is always important.

The revolutionary, however, is part of a movement, not a heroic individual. Hugo took part in a pre-existing *campesino* movement in Cusco. He was often the individual face of the uprising, but dozens of others were involved in organising, and thousands played a part. The masses make history. Participation is everything, and successful movements harness the creativity of millions. Nonetheless, collective strength can be conserved and enhanced through practical solidarity for individuals under threat from the authorities for their militancy. The Irish revolutionary Bobby Sands, who died in 1981 after 66 days on hunger strike, suggested 'Everyone, Republican or otherwise has his or her own particular part to play. No part is too great or too small, no one is too old or too young to do something.' (Sands in Dowler 1998: 169–170)

## Strategies for survival

Some on the left put their faith in electoral politics, yet success in elections has so far failed to create socialist or ecosocialist societies. Examples of co-option are numerous, it's not necessarily that bad people seek office and betray movements, although this does occur. More fundamentally, with entrenched power structures, those in office may be more shaped by the system than able to shape it. In Greece, the left-wing Syriza, a party sympathetic to ecosocialism, ended up continuing a path of austerity (Sheehan 2017). Nonetheless, electoral politics is part of political change and non–electoral alternatives have also tended to fail. Both the indigenous and the Trotskyist strands in Hugo Blanco's story have stressed resistance, rather than taking electoral office. His personal experience of electoral politics was at best mixed. However while he promotes the Zapatista approaching of building alternative structures, which shares similar elements with the notion of dual power, he does not engage in sectarian denunciation of those who take the electoral path. In 2013 he argued:

the principal task is not to elect to parliament comrades who in many cases will be corrupted by their huge salaries or will be too small a minority to introduce laws favourable to the people. We are not calling for a boycott of elections, as that is another battle that can be discussed. Rather, we are not convinced that electoral politics should be our main task.

We are of course interested in unity of the left during elections, in the understanding that a fundamental part of its program must be a condemnation of the successive right-wing governments' subservience to the transnationals, together with unconditional support for the people's struggle in defense of water and the environment. (Blanco 2013a)

Green Parties, since the dispute between 'fundamentalist' and 'realos' in the 1980s, have perhaps largely ignored this question of the effectiveness of electoral politics as a path to social change (Doherty 1992). In Latin America, in contrast, fierce debate has ensued. Marta Harnecker, the Chilean sociologist, has suggested that social movement mobilisation needs an electoral dimension. She argues that, to make the 'impossible possible', it is necessary, although insufficient, to win elections (Harnecker 2007). Summarizing many critical voices, Jeffrey Webber argues that electoral victories have seen left governments maintain extractivist policies, demobilize social movements and continue within a capitalist economic structure. He has called for dual power, a more indigenous form of Marxism inspired by Mariátegui, and suggested that the Latin American left governments may have fallen into a Stalinist 'stageist' approach. By this, he means that they argue for economic growth and industrialisation, basically within capitalism, as a stage necessary before the transition to ecosocialism (Webber 2017b: 110).

Hugo's position is quite nuanced, he has most sympathy for the Zapatista alternative of building community power, but he argues that in some circumstances electoral politics may be useful. It is worth noting that he was able to work closely with Javier Diez Canseco in the PUM (*Partido Unificado Mariateguista*). Javier perceived a dual role of the left party, participating in elections but building community alternatives. Aware of the danger that a left party might act as a *colchón* (mattress), a buffer between the establishment and the people, he stressed the need to organise at the grassroots level (Schönwälder 2002: 100). The PUM was strongly supportive of the CCP and took part with Hugo Blanco as a leading member of both, in the land occupations in Puno (Blanco 2018a: 86). Hugo mourned his comrade when he died in 2013:

The popular struggles in which he participated bring us closer to the one way open to us to ward off extinction: Self-government by the people, displacing big multinational capital from the seat of power.

He took important steps forward in this respect. With his exceptional skill in navigating through the corrupt Peruvian parliament, he succeeded in sending a former minister to prison. As we walk the streets of Lima and other cities and see the ramps built to aid those with disabilities, we should bear in mind that they wouldn't be there if not for Javier. (Blanco 2013b)

Hugo stresses popular mobilisation but notes on occasions that electoral politics can be productive. He does suggest that, where the electoral alternatives fail, the Zapatista strategy is a viable path. No strategy, though, provides an easy road to transcending a capitalist system. Hugo has, to repeat, suggested a diversity of tactics may be relevant and that close attention to context is necessary.

Ecosocialism suggests that transcending capitalism is necessary to our survival as a species. It is also a matter of respecting and protecting the diversity of forms of life we coexist with on Planet Earth. Michael Löwy, a prominent academic and member of the Fourth International, advocates ecosocialism by referencing Walter Benjamin:

Marx said that revolutions are the locomotive of world history. But perhaps things are very different. It may be that revolutions are the act by which the human race travelling in the train applies the emergency brake. (Benjamin in Löwy 2005: 66-76)

Hugo Blanco has been a consistently practical and militant ecosocialist revolutionary. His life and thought provide an excellent starting point for developing strategies of resistance and transformation necessary to pull on the brakes, to halt the destruction of nature. Hugo has set an example. We need to set an example too.

# Acronyms

AIDESEP *Asociación Interétnica de Desarrollo de la Selva Peruana* (Inter-ethnic Association for the Development of the Peruvian Rainforest)

AP *Acción Popular* (Popular Action)

APRA *Alianza Popular Revolucionaria* (American Popular Revolutionary Alliance)

CCP *Confederación Campesina del Peru* (Peru Peasants Federation)

CGTP *Confederación General de Trabajadores Peruanos* (General Confederation of Peruvian Workers)

CODDEH *Comité de Defensa de los Derechos Humanos* (Committee for the Defence of Human Rights)

DSA Democratic Socialists of America

ELN *Ejército de Liberación Nacional* (Army of National Liberation)  Peru

FDCC *La Federación Departamental de Campesinos del Cusco* (Regional Federation of the Campesinos of Cusco)

FEPCACYL *La Federación Provincial de Campesinos de La Convención, Yanityle y Lares* (Peasants Federation La Convención, Yanityle y Lares)

FIR *Frente de Izquierda Revolucionaria* (Left Revolutionary Front) Peru

FOCEP *Frente Obrero, Campesino, Estudiantil, y Popular* (Workers, Peasants, Students, and Popular Front)

FPCC *Federación Departamental de Campesinos del Cusco* (Peasant Federation of Cusco)

FTC *Federación Departamental de Trabajadores del Cusco* (Workers' Federation of Cusco)

GOM *Grupo Obrero Marxista* (Marxist Workers Group) Argentina, Peru

ICFI International Committee of the Fourth International

IS International Socialists

MIR *Movimiento de Izquierda Revolucionaria* (Left Revolutionary Movement) Peru, Chile

MOVADEF *Movimiento por la Amnistía y los Derechos Fundamentales* (Movement for Amnesty and Fundamental Rights)

MPT *Movimiento de los Pueblos y los Trabajadores* (People and Workers' Movement) MPT Chile

MRTA *Movimiento Revolucionario Túpac Amaru* (Túpac Amaru Revolutionary Movement) Peru

PIC *Plataforma Interinstitucional de Celendín* (Celendina Inter-institutional Platform)

PIP Peruvian Investigations Police

POR *Partido Obrero Revolucionario* (Revolutionary Workers' Party) Peru

PPC *Partido Comunista del Perú* (Peruvian Communist Party)

PPC-SL *Partido Comunista del Perú - Sendero Luminoso* (Peruvian Communist Party – Shining Path)

PRT *Partido Revolucionario de los Trabajadores* (Workers' Revolutionary Party)

PSR *Partido Socialista Revolucionario* (Revolutionary Socialist Party)

PST *Partido Socialista de los Trabajadores* (Socialist Workers Party) Peru

PUM *Partido Unificado Mariateguista* (Unified Mariátegui Party) Peru

SCCh *Sindicato de Campesinos de Chaupimayo* (Union of Chaupimayo Peasants)

SLATO Latin American Secretariat of Orthodox Trotskyism

SWP Socialist Workers Party, US

UDP *Unidad Democrática Popular* (Democratic People's Union)

UL *Izquierda Unida* (United Left)

USFI United Secretariat of the Fourth International

USLA US Committee for Justice to Latin American Political Prisoners

# Glossary

*Allegados* Sub tenants of *Arrendires*

*Amauta* Wise teacher

*Arrendires* Tenants

*Ayllu* Andean commons or community

*Campesino* Peasant

*Gamonal* Landowner

*Hacienda* A large estate

*Huayno* A type of song from the Andes

*Huelga* An indefinite strike or work stoppage

*Indio sonqo* Indian Heart

*Lucha Indigena* Indigenous Struggle (Hugo's newspaper)

*Misti* Non-indigenous person

*Pachamama* The earth goddess

*Paro* A short strike or work stoppage, often for a single day

*P'ata kiskas* Cactus

*Puna* Grass covered plains

*Ronda campesinas* Peasant self-defence committees

*Selva* The rainforest

*Sierra* Mountains

*Tawantinsuyu* The Four Regions, the Quechua term for what the Spanish called the Inca Empire

*Tayta* Wise father

*Yunsa* a traditional dance festival controversial because it involves tree cutting

# Bibliography

Alexander, R. (1973) *Trotskyism in Latin America*. Stanford: Hoover Institution Press.

Anderson, B. (1983) *Imagined Communities: Reflections on the Origin and Spread of Nationalism*. London: Verso.

Anon (1963a) 'News about Hugo Blanco', *The Internationalist*, Feb 5, 1963, p. 3.

Anon (1963b) 'Free Hugo Blanco', *The Internationalist*, May 1963, p. 5.

Anon (1963c) 'N.Y. Pickets to Ask: "Free Hugo Blanco"', *The Militant*, 27, 27: 1.

Anon (1963d) 'FIR Bulletin Appears in Buenos Aires', *World Outlook*, 1, 18: 14-15.

Anon (1964) 'Hugo Blanco's Sister Arrested', *World Outlook*, 2, 11: 1.

Anon (1966) 'Hugo Blanco's Codefendants ask Death Penalty, too, if he is to be shot', *World Outlook,* 4, 39: 1.

Anon (1967a) 'Meeting held for Hugo Blanco in London', *World Outlook,* 5, 25: 649.

Anon (1967b) 'Peruvian Military Court Spares Hugo Blanco's life', *World Outlook*, 5, 34: 861.

Anon (1968) 'Life in El Frontón', *World Outlook,* 6, 16: 376.

Anon (1971a) 'Campaign for Hugo Blanco Ends in Great Victory', *Intercontinental Press,* 9, 1: 3-4.

Anon (1971b) 'General's Impose Ban on Hugo Blanco', *Intercontinental Press*, 9, 4: 78.

Anon (1972a) 'Hugo Blanco Leaves Mexico', *Intercontinental Press* 10, 27: 804.

Anon (1972b) 'Hugo Blanco Fights to Remain in Argentina', *Intercontinental Press* 10, 31: 923.

Anon (1972c) 'Hugo Blanco Leaves Argentina for Chile', *Intercontinental Press* 10, 41: 1249.

Anon (1973) 'Hugo Blanco Arrives in Sweden from Chile', *Intercontinental Press* 11, 41: 1327.

Anon (1974) 'Hugo Blanco and Hector Bejor Cross Swords', *Intercontinental Press,* 12, no. 39: 1434-1436.

Anon (1976a) 'Hugo Blanco Cheered on Return to Peru', *Intercontinental Press,* 14, 2: 46.

Anon (1976b) 'Hugo Blanco Harassed by Police and Maoists', *Intercontinental Press,* 14, 213: 951.

Anon (1978a) 'Martial Law Declared in Peru', *Intercontinental Press,* 16, 21: 628.

Anon (1978b) 'Hugo Blanco Deported', *Intercontinental Press,* 16, 22: 661.

Anon (1978c) 'Save the Life of Hugo Blanco!', *Intercontinental Press,* 16, 23: 693.

Anon (1978d) '*Dagens Nyheter* interviews Hugo Blanco', *Intercontinental Press,* 16, 17: 500-501.

Anon (1979) 'Hugo Blanco 'Man of the Year', *Intercontinental Press,* 17, 1: 15.

Anon (2016) 'Peru: The Hugo Blanco Galdos School for Environmental and Social Leaders', *War on Want.* < https://waronwant.org/media/peru-hugo-blanco-galdos-school-environmental-and-social-leaders>

Anon (2017) 'Italy Convicts Eight South Americans in Plan Condor Trial', *BBC,* 18 January <www.bbc.co.uk/news/world-latin-america-38659230>

Anon (2018) 'Kerala Floods: Troops rush in to help rescue efforts', *BBC,* 18 August <www.bbc.co.uk/news/world-asia-india-45231222>

Arguedas, J. (1992) *Deep Rivers.* Austin. Texas: University of Texas Press.

Beauvais, J-P. (1980) 'Hugo Blanco Elected to Congress in Peru', *Intercontinental Press* 18, 2: 562.

Béjar, H. (1970) *Peru 1965: Notes on a Guerrilla Experience.* New York: Monthly Review Press.

Bel, P. (2017) 'Qué es el Movadef, la Polémica Organización que Vinculan con Sendero Luminoso en Perú y a la que acusan de Apología al Terrorismo', *BBC Mundo,* 9 August <https://www.bbc.com/mundo/noticias-america-latina-40856626>

Berglund, O. (2008) 'Hugo Blanco arrested for Supporting Farmers' Struggle', *International Viewpoint.* <http://www.internationalviewpoint.org/spip.php?article1536>

Bethell, L. (1993) *Chile Since Independence.* Cambridge: Cambridge University Press.

Blanco, H. (1962) 'Interview', *Expreso*, 21 May 1962, p.8.

Blanco, H. (1965) 'On Guerrilla Fighters and Militias', *World Outlook*, 3, 8: 11–14.

Blanco, H. (1968) 'Hugo Blanco denounces murder of prisoners in El Frontón', *Intercontinental Press,* 6, 33: 838.

Blanco, H. (1971a) 'Exclusive interview with Hugo Blanco', *The Militant,* 19 March 1971, pp. 12–14.

Blanco, H. (1971b) ' Hugo Blanco Describes His Expulsion From Peru,' *Intercontinental Press,* 9, 33: 809–810.

Blanco, H. (1971c) 'Hugo Blanco Explains Why He Was Exiled', *Intercontinental Press,* 9, 34: 832–833.

Blanco, H. (1972) 'Which Way for Peru, Uruguay, and Chile?', *Intercontinental Press,* 10, 2: 36–40.

Blanco, H. (1973) 'Fascist Provocations, Labor Unrest in Chile', *Intercontinental Press* 11, 21: 667–668.

Blanco, H. (1974) 'On the Situation in Latin America', *Intercontinental Press*, 12, 28: 990–992.

Blanco, H. (1975a) 'The Fight Against Repression', *International Socialist Review*, September 5, pp. 13–19.

Blanco, H. (1975b) 'Why Kissinger Won't Let Me Speak in the United States', *Intercontinental Press,* 13, 39: 1490–1491.

Blanco, H. (1977) *Land or Death: the Peasant Struggle in Peru.* New York: Pathfinder Press.

Blanco, H. (1978) *'Workers and Peasants to Power!': A Revolutionary Program for Peru.* New York: Pathfinder Press.

Blanco, H. (1979) 'Hugo Blanco Hails Advances of Revolution in Nicaragua', *Intercontinental Press*, 17, 35: 920–921.

Blanco, H. (1984) 'Left Unity and Sendero Luminoso', *Intercontinental Press*, 22, 5: 154–157.

Blanco, H. (1993) 'The Environmentalism of the People', *Against the Current* 42. <https://www.marxists.org/history/etol/newspape/atc/5004.html>

Blanco, H. (2003) 'Hugo Blanco Greets Congress', *International Viewpoint*, <http://internationalviewpoint.org/spip.php?article231>

Blanco, H. (2008a) *The Fight for Indigenous Rights in the Andes Today.* Toronto: Socialist Voice.

Blanco, H. (2008b) `No Contradiction Between my Indigenous Struggle and Dialectical materialism', *Links International Journal of Socialist Renewal* <http://links.org.au/node/696>

Blanco, H. (2008c) 'Permanent Resistance to Oppression', *Lucha Indigena*, 26: 2.

Blanco, H. (2010a) 'Foreword' in Wall, D. *The Rise of the Green Left*. London: Pluto Press.

Blanco, H. (2010b) 'To Save the Human Race', *Lucha Indigena*, 45: 2.

Blanco, H. (2011a) 'Elections', *Lucha Indigena,* 56: 2.

Blanco, H. (2011b) 'Two Irreconcilable Undertakings', *Lucha Indigena* 62: 2.

Blanco, H (2013a) 'Cañaris: The War Against the People Goes on',

*Lucha Indigena* 78: 2.

Blanco, H. (2013b) 'Javier', *Lucha Indigena*, 82: .2.

Blanco, H. (2014a) 'The Indigenous Movements are Building the New Society' in Ross, C. and Rein, M. *Until the Rulers Obey: Voices from the Latin American Social Movements*. Oakland, California: PM Press.

Blanco, H. (2014b) 'Big capital is eliminating surplus populations', *Lucha Indigena* 93: 2.

Blanco, H. (2015a) 'Terrorism from above and from below feed on each other', *Lucha Indigena,* 112: 2.

Blanco, H. (2015b) 'Hugo Blanco llama a Votar por Verónika Mendoza y el Frente Amplio',*Servindi* <www.servindi.org/actualidad/146159>

Blanco, H. (2018a) *We the Indians: the Indigenous Peoples of Peru and the Struggle for Land*. London: Merlin Press.

Blanco, H. (2018b) '8 March, International Women's Day', *Lucha Indigena,* 140: 2.

Bollinger, W. (1978) 'Peru: The Left Gathers Force', *North American Congress on Latin America Report,* 12, 5: 44 – 46.

Bookchin, M. (1993) *Deep Ecology & Anarchism: A Polemic*. London: Freedom Press.

Brass, T. (1989) 'Trotskyism, Hugo Blanco and the Ideology of a Peruvian Peasant movement.' *The Journal of Peasant Studies,* 16, 2: 173–197.

Brass, T. (2017) 'Viva La Revolución? Reassessing Hobsbawm on Peasants', *Critique of Anthropology* 37, 3: 244-261.

Brecht, B. (1964) 'A Short Organum for the Theatre' in Willett, J. *Brecht on Theatre: The Development of an Aesthetic*. London: Methuen.

Camejo, P. (2010) *North Star: A Memoir*. Chicago, Illinois: Haymarket Books.

Chambers, S. and Chasteen, J. (2010) *Latin American Independence: An Anthology of Sources*. Indianapolis: Hackett Publishing Company.

Cheyre, E. (2013) 'Characteristics of and Influences on the Armed Forces during Democratic Transition' in Blair *Latin American Military Engagement: Influencing Armed Forces Worldwide to Support Democratic Transitions*. Washington, D.C: Brookings Institution Press.

Ciccariello-Maher, G. (2013) *We Created Chávez: A People's History of the Venezuelan Revolution*. Durham, North Carolina: Duke University Press.

Conaghan, C. (2005) *Fujimori's Peru: Deception in the Public Sphere*, Pennsylvania: University of Pittsburgh Press.

Cone, K. (2000) *Disability Rights and Independent Living Movement Oral History Series. Online Archive of California*. University of California. <https://oac.cdlib.org/ark:/13030/kt1w1001mt/?brand=oac4>

Cooper, H. (1969) Peru's Island Prison of El Frontón, *International Journal of Offender Therapy and Comparative Criminology*, 13, 3: 183-187.

Craig, W. (1969) 'Peru: The Peasant Movement of La Convención' in Landsberger, H. *Latin American Peasant Movements*. Ithaca, NY: Cornell University Press.

Debray, R. (1975) *Che's Guerilla War*. Harmondsworth: Penguin.

De Castro, E. (2016) *The Relative Native: Essays on Indigenous Conceptual Worlds*. Chicago, Illinois: University of Chicago Press.

Degregori, C. (1992) 'A Dwarf Star', *North American Congress on Latin America Report* 24, 4: 44-46.

Degregori, C. (2012) *How Difficult it is to be God: Shining Path's Politics of War in Peru, 1980-1999*. Madison: The University of Wisconsin Press.

De La Cadena, M. (2015) *Earth Beings: Ecologies of Practice Across Andean Worlds*. Durham, North Carolina: Duke University Press.

Deutscher, I. (1954) *The Prophet Armed: Trotsky, 1879-1921*. Oxford: Oxford University Press.Doherty, B. (1992) 'The Fundi Realo Controversy: An analysis of four European green parties', *Environmental Politics*, 1, 1: 95-120.

Dosal, P. (1993) *Doing Business With the Dictators: A Political History of United Fruit in Guatemala, 1899–1944*. London: Rowman & Littlefield.

Dowler, L. (1998) 'And They Think I'm Just a Nice Old Lady' Women and War in Belfast, Northern Ireland', *Gender, Place & Culture*, 5:2, 159-176.

Elbaum, M. (2018) *Revolution in the Air: Sixties Radicals turn to Lenin, Mao and Che*. London: Verso.

Feldman, I. (2014) *Rethinking Community From Peru: The Political Philosophy of José María Arguedas*. Pennsylvania: University of Pittsburgh Press.

Feuer, L. (1969) *The Conflict of Generations: the Character and Significance of Student Movements*. New York: Basic Books.

Fourth International (1996) 'Our International', *International Viewpoint*, <*http://internationalviewpoint.org/spip.php?article351*>

Fraser, N. and Navarro, M. (1997) *Evita: The Real Lives of Eva Peron*. London: Andre Deutsch.

Gall, N. (1964) 'Letter from Peru', *Commentary*. June 1964, pp. 64-69.

Gall, N. (1967) 'Peru's Misfired Guerrilla Campaign', *The Reporter*, January 26, 1967, p. 36.

Galeano, E. (1997) *Open Veins of Latin America: Five Centuries of the Pillage of a Continent*. New York: NYU Press.

Galeano, E. (2013) *Children of the Days: A Calendar of Human History*. London: Penguin.

Galeano, E. (2018) 'Foreward' in Blanco, H. *We the Indians: the Indigenous Peoples of Peru and the Struggle for Land*. London: Merlin Press.

Gott, R. (1973) *Rural Guerrillas in Latin America*. Harmondsworth: Penguin Books.

Greenland, H. (1998) *Red Hot: the Life & Times of Nick Origlass, 1908-1996*. Sydney: Wellington Lane Press.

Hamilton, E. (2017) 'The Future is Indigenous', *Guernica*, 11 December. < https://www.guernicamag.com/hugo-blanco-future-indigenous-climate-change/>

Hand, M. (2018) 'Native Americans who protested Dakota Access get handed the longest prison sentences', *Think Progress* <https://thinkprogress. org/native-americans-who-protested-dakota-access-get-handed-the-longest-prison-sentences-e7510ca5f2d7/>

Handelman, H. (1975) *Struggle in the Andes: Peasant Political Mobilization in Peru*. Austin: University of Texas Press.

Hansen, J. (1979) *The Leninist Strategy of Party Building: the Debate on Guerrilla Warfare in Latin America*. New York: Pathfinder Press.

Harnecker, M. (2007) *Building the Left*. Zed: London.

Harvey, N. (1995) 'Rebellion in Chiapas: Rural Reforms and Popular Struggle', *Third World Quarterly* 16, 1: 39-73.

Heilman, J. (2000) Leader and Led: Hugo Blanco, La Convención Peasants, and the Relationships of Revolution. Master's thesis. University of Wisconsin – Madison.

Hobsbawm, E. (1969) 'A Case of Neo-Feudalism: La Convención, Peru', *Journal of Latin American Studies* 1, 1: 31–50.

Hofman, P. (1975) 'President of Peru Ousted In Coup Led by the Military', *New York Times*, 30 August.

Holmberg, M. (1976)' The Masses Have Realized How Little Has Changed' *Intercontinental Press*, 14, 11: 441.

Huilca, P. (2012) 'La Reinvención de Hugo Blanco', *La República* <https://larepublica.pe/archivo/613190-la-reinvencion-de-hugo-blanco>

Hunefeldt, C. (2004) *A Brief History of Peru*. New York: Lexington.

Jameson, F. (1975) *The Prison-House of Language A Critical Account of Structuralism and Russian Formalism*. Princeton, New Jersey: Princeton University Press.

John, S. (2009) *Bolivia's Radical Tradition: Permanent Revolution in the Andes*. Tucson, Arizona: University of Arizona Press.

Kelly, J. (2018) *Contemporary Trotskyism: Parties, Sects and Social Movements in Britain*. London: Routledge.

Klein, N. (2018) 'Capitalism Killed Our Climate Momentum, Not 'Human Nature'. *The Intercept* <https://theintercept.com/2018/08/03/climate-change-new-york-times-magazine/>

Knapp, M., Flach, A., Ayboga, E. and Abdullah, A. (2016) *Rojava Revolution: Democratic Autonomy and Women's Liberation in Syrian Kurdistan*. London: Pluto Press.

Lambright, A. (2010) *Creating the Hybrid Intellectual: Subject, Space and the Feminine in the Narratives of José María Arguedas*. New Jersey: Associated University Presses.

Lenin, V. (1964 [1917]) ' Dual Power' in *Lenin Collected Works*, Moscow: Progress Publishers, 24: 38–41.

Liszt, G. (2018) Who was Nahuel Moreno? *Left Voice* <http://www.leftvoice.org/Who-was-Nahuel-Moreno>

Loveman, B. and Davies, T. (1985) 'Case Studies of Guerrilla Movements and Political Change', in *Guerrilla Warfare: Che Guevarra*, Lincoln: University of Nebraska Press.

Löwy, M. (1981) *The Politics of Combined and Uneven Development: the Theory of Permanent Revolution*. London: New Left Books.

Löwy, M. (1992) *Marxism in Latin America from 1909 to the Present: an Anthology*. Atlantic Highlands, New Jersey: Humanities Press.

Löwy, M. (2005) *Fire Alarm: Reading Walter Benjamin's On the Concept of History*. London: Verso.

Löwy, M. (2015) *Ecosocialism: A Radical Alternative to Capitalist Catastrophe*. Chicago, Illinois: Haymarket Books.

Mac Ionnrachtaigh, F. (2013) *Language, Resistance and Revival Republican Prisoners and the Irish Language in the North of Ireland*. London: Pluto Press.

Maitan, L. (1965) 'The Revolt of the Peruvian Campesinos,' *International Socialist Review* 26, 2: 38-41.

Martínez-Alier, J. (2001) *The Environmentalism of the Poor: A Study of Ecological Conflicts and Valuation*. Cheltenham: Edward Elgar.

Montag, W. (1998) 'Preface' in Balibar, E. *Spinoza and Politics*. London: Verso.

Morañ, M. (2016) *Arguedas / Vargas Llosa: Dilemmas and Assemblages*. London: Palgrave Macmillan.

Murphy, F. (1978a) 'International Protests Free Hugo Blanco', *Intercontinental Press* 16, 25: 756-757.

Murphy, F. (1978b) 'Hugo Blanco Elected to Peru Constituent Assembly', *Intercontinental Press,* 16, 26: 788-790.

Muscutt, K. (1999) *Warriors of the Clouds: A Lost Civilization in the Upper Amazon of Peru*. Albuquerque: University of New Mexico Press.

Næss, A. (1973) 'The Shallow and the Deep, Long-Range Ecology Movement. A Summary', *Inquiry*, 16: 95-100.

Neira, H. (1964) *Cuzco: Tierra y Muerte*. Cuzco: Problemas de Hoy.

Nyblom, B. (1973) 'Workers in Front Lines in Latin America', *Intercontinental Press* 11, 34: 1089-1090.

Olivera, R. (2011) 'Hugo Blanco' *New Internationalist*, 1 January < <https://newint.org/columns/makingwaves/2011/01/01/indigenous-rights-hugo-blanco>

Ostrom, E. (1990) *Governing the Commons: The evolution of Institutions for Collective Action*. Cambridge: Cambridge University Press.

Pärssinen, M. (1992) *Tawantinsuyu: the Inca State and its Political Organization*. Helsinki, Finland: The Finnish Historical Society.

Poole, D. and Rénique, G. (1992) *Peru – Time of Fear*. London: Latin American Bureau.

Rai, M. (2017) 'The Nonviolent Russian Revolution', *Peace News*. Issue 2610-2611    <www.peacenews.info/node/8820/nonviolent-russian-revolution>

Raptis, M. (1974) *Revolution and Counter Revolution in Chile: A Dossier on Workers' Participation in the Revolutionary Process*. London: Allison and Busby.

Roberts, A. (1979) *The Self-Managing Environment*. London: Alison and Busby.

Roberts, P. (1998) *Deepening Democracy? The Modern Left and Social Movements in Chile and Peru*. Stanford, California: Stanford University Press.

Rosemont, F. (2009) 'Karl Marx and the Iroquois', < http://www.libcom .org/library/karl-marx-iroquois-franklin-rosemont>

Ross, C. and Rein, M. (2014) *Until the Rulers Obey: Voices from Latin American Social Movements*. Oakland, California: PM Press.

Ross, T. (1973) 'Old allies turning against Allende', *Guardian*, 12 August.    <https://www.theguardian.com/world/1973/aug/12/chile. fromthearchive>

Roxborough, I., O'Brien, P. and Roddick, J. (1977) *Chile: The State and Revolution*. London: Macmillan.

Saul, Q. (2015) 'From Indigenous Struggle to Ecosocialism', *Counterpunch* 19 May <https://www.counterpunch.org/2015/05/19/from-indigenous-struggle-to-ecosocialism/≥

Schönwälder, G. (2002) *Linking Civil Society and the State: Urban Popular Movements, the Left, and Local Government in Peru, 1980–1992*. Pennsylvania: Penn State Press.

Schlesinger, S. and Kinzer, S. (1983) *Bitter Fruit: The Untold Story of the American Coup in Guatemala*. New York: Anchor Books.

Seligmann, L. (1995) *Between Reform and Revolution: Political Struggles in the Peruvian Andes, 1969-1991*. Stanford, California: Stanford University Press.

Shady, R., Haas, J. and Creamer, W. (2001) 'Dating Caral, a Pre-ceramic Site in the Supe Valley on the Central Coast of Peru', *Science*, 292: 723-726.

Shantz, J. (2012) *Green Syndicalism: An Alternative Red/Green Vision*. New York: Syracuse University Press.

Sheehan, H. (2017) *Syriza Wave: Surging and Crashing with the Greek Left*. New York: NYU Press.

Socialist Resistance (2009) 'From the other side of the world, Hugo Blanco thanks the Vestas workers.' 23 July, http://socialistresistance.org/from-the-other-side-of-the-world-hugo-blanco-thanks-the-vestas-workers/622.

Soyinka, W. (1990) 'Twice Bitten: The Fate of Africa's Culture Producers', *Publications of the Modern Language Association of America,* 105, 1: 110-120.

Starn, O. (1999) *Nightwatch: The Politics of Protest in the Andes.* Durham, North Carolina: Duke University Press.

Stolze, E. (2017) 'Review of Jason Read: The Politics of Transindividuality', *Human Studies* 40, 4: 707-711.

Taylor, L. (2006) *Shining Path: Guerrilla War in Peru's Northern Highlands, 1980-1997.* Liverpool: Liverpool University Press.

Thompson, E.P. (1975) *Whigs and Hunters: The Origin of the Black Act.* New York: Pantheon Books.

Thornett, A. (2010) 'Fourth International declares itself ecosocialist', *Socialist Resistance,* 5 March < http://socialistresistance.org/fourth-international-declares-itself-ecosocialist/870>.

Thornett, A. Arguments for Ecosocialism, (forthcoming) Resistance Books

Thorstad, D. (1972) 'Hugo Blanco Jailed Without Charge in Argentina', *Intercontinental Press* 10, 30: 883.

Trotsky, L. (1955) *Literature and Revolution.* New York: Russell and Russell.

Trotsky, L. (1980) *The Balkan Wars.* New York: Pathfinder Press.

Trotsky, L. (2007 [1906]) *The Permanent Revolution and Results and Prospects.* London: Resistance Books.

Trotsky, L. (2017 [1932]) *A History of the Russian Revolution.* London: Penguin.

Vanden, H. and Becker, M. (2011) *José Carlos Mariátegui: An Anthology.* New York: Monthly Review Press.

Villanueva, V. (1967) *Hugo Blanco y la Rebelión Campesina.* Lima: Librería-Editorial J. Mejía Baca.

Wall, D. (2005) *Babylon and Beyond: The Economics of Anti-Capitalist, Anti-Globalist and Radical Green Movements.* London: Pluto Press.

Wall, D. (2010) *The Rise of the Green Left.* London: Pluto Press.

Wall, D. (2014a) *The Commons in History.* Cambridge, Massachusetts: MIT Press.

Wall, D. (2014b) *The Sustainable Economics of Elinor Ostrom.* London: Routledge.

Wall, D. (2017) *Elinor Ostrom's Rules for Radicals.* London: Pluto Press.

Ward, A. (2011) 'An Interview with Hugo Blanco', *Interventions,* 13, 4: 651-663.

Webber, J. (2017a) 'Assessing the Pink Tide', *Jacobin* <www.jacobinmag.com/2017/04/lula-correa-rousseff-left-pink-tide>

Webber, J. (2017b) *The Last Days of Oppression and the First Day of the Same: The Politics and Economics of the New Latin American Left.* Chicago, Illinois: Haymarket Books.

Weinberg, W. (2002) *Homage to Chiapas: The New Indigenous Struggles in Mexico.* London: Verso.

Weinberg, W. (2009) 'Peru: Veteran Guerilla Fighter Hugo Blanco Speaks on Amazon Struggle', *CounterVortex.* <https://countervortex.org/node/7756>

Werlich, D. (1978) *Peru: A Short History.* Carbondale, Illinois.: Southern Illinois University Press.

White, J. (1976) 'Hugo Blanco Deported to Sweden', *Intercontinental Press*, 14, 28: 1092.

Zevallos, M. (2017) 'Hugo Blanco, Historia de Lucha y Rebeldía', *Gran Angular.* 12 June < elgranangular.com/blog/entrevista/hugo-blanco-historia-de-lucha-y-rebeldi>

# INDEX

# ALSO AVAILABLE FROM THE MERLIN PRESS

## WE THE INDIANS

*The indigenous peoples of Peru and the struggle for land*
by Hugo Blanco
With a foreword by Eduardo Galeano

Hugo Blanco is a historic leader of the Peruvian campesino struggle and a key figure in the huge insurrections of the rural dispossessed.

He was a key protagonist in the stories he shares in vivid but direct language. At the same time he gives voice to those who fought alongside him, while always advocating a respectful relationship with Pacamama (Mother Earth).

*A red thread runs through these beautiful, scattered reflections, polemical interventions, autobiographical vignettes, and letters – Hugo Blanco's unwavering stand with the oppressed, and belief in their capacity for selfemancipation. Jailed, exiled, tortured, his spirit of sedition never seems to wane. From student militancy, to factory organizing, to mobilizing with the landless, Blanco's first political decades in Peru and Argentina set on course a long life of resolute antagonism to the tyranny of capital across several continents.*
– Jeffery R. Webber, author of The Last Day of Oppression, and the First Day of the Same: The Politics and Economics of the New Latin American Left

*Hugo Blanco is an inspiration. There are many lessons we can derive from the vivid tales narrated so accessibly in this book.*
Derek Wall, former principal speaker of the Green Party of England and Wales. His most recent book is *Elinor Ostrom's Rules for Radicals*

With 15 woodcuts

ISBN 978-0-85036-738-6 paperback

## www.merlinpress.co.uk